ALL MY PEOPLE ARE ELEGIES

Essays, Prose Poems and Other Epistolary Oddities

Other Books by Sean Thomas Dougherty

Not All Saints
Alongside We Travel: Contemporary Poets on Autism
The Second O of Sorrow
Double Kiss: Stories, Poems and Essays on the Art of Billiards
All You Ask for Is Longing
Sasha Sings the Laundry on the Line
Scything Grace
The Blue City
Broken Hallelujahs
Maria Mazziotti Gillan: Essays on Her Works
Nightshift Belonging to Lorca
Along the Lake: Contemporary Writing from Erie, PA
The Biography of Broken Things
Except by Falling
The Body's Precarious Balance
Love Song of the Young Couple, The Dumb Job
The Mercy of Sleep

ALL MY PEOPLE ARE ELEGIES

Essays, Prose Poems and Other Epistolary Oddities

by

Sean Thomas Dougherty

The New York Quarterly Foundation, Inc.
Beacon, New York

NYQ Books™ is an imprint of The New York Quarterly Foundation, Inc.

The New York Quarterly Foundation, Inc.
P. O. Box 470
Beacon, NY 12508

www.nyq.org

First Edition

Set in New Baskerville

Layout and Design by Raymond P. Hammond

Cover Photogaph: "Lensball on Lincoln Street" by Danny Rebb Fine Art Photography

Author Photograph by Andy Denial

Library of Congress Control Number: 2019947599

ISBN: 978-1-63045-072-4

For Lisa, my last love, my first editor

And to all the editors on this planet
up all night

reading through the work
of strangers

Contents

ALL MY PEOPLE ARE ELEGIES

Essays, Prose Poems and Other Epistolary Oddities

Dear Editors of Esteemed and Tiny Journals,

I know how hard you work for nothing but the love of the art, and how underappreciated you often are, so I have attached no poems for submission, thereby saving you the time of reading them, time that could be better spent reading the better poems of others, or spending time with your lover or your children, or simply sitting in the sun and maybe even writing a poem of your own, one I hope will not receive the sadness of the consequent form rejection that you would have sent if I had included my poems, poems that would have kept you from that party you were going to blow off in order to catch up on the hundreds of submissions clogging your In-Box. Now you can take that subway ride, where you can nod your head with your eyes closed and your earplugs on, listening to that obscure composer you love of sonatas for cello and sousaphone. For the world is rather like the bell of a Sousaphone, or is it love that is the bell? The one ringing now in the high cathedral on the far side of town, where there had only been funerals for the last decade. Where the coffins are cloaked with sunflowers. The old Bulgarian women are donning their black netting. Oh Editor, where are the weddings? Who is writing, as Lorca asks, the Baptism of the new? No, my poems are not, they are old as dust, or dirt, or a broom. Too many of us are bothering you. Turn off your computer, dear Editor. There is honey waiting to be spooned in your tea. There is poppyseed cake. Look out the window. There is wild thyme and fennel.

Sincerely,

Dear Editor of Esteemed Midwestern Journal,

I am sorry to bother you again. No, I have not attached poems for submission. Instead I wanted to tell you about the smell of beer and fried food at Wrigley Field when my friend Michael was a boy, and the scent of pierogi his mother baked, and the South Side blues that rang from the high window of a girl in her room reciting to herself, who would grow up to blow the mic off every stiff podium. I wanted to remind you of Lake Michigan frozen, and the ice fishers huddled over their chain-sawed holes, and the razored wind that rips into the aluminum walls of freight cars that men are loading with gloved hands. I am writing to tell you that last night I worked the night shift and I stood over an old man I take care of praying, I was praying he was breathing. He was. But every night I ask you how many of us are praying to simply breathe?

Sincerely,

Dear Editor Sipping Wine the Color of Posh,

I've been worrying about you because I read on your guidelines that you receive over 10,000 submissions. Just reading that made me want to pop a handful of Tylenol PM and then sit in a chair and stare at the light on the wall. It is oddly warm today, is it warm where you are over in the Midwest? I checked the weather channel and I hope you are not in the rain from the leftover hurricane, as if the hurricane is something we could eat with a giant spoon, not the little spoons too many of my dead used to burn with their lighter and keep in a kit they'd hide in a hole in the wall. Oh editor, I sometimes wonder if not all what we write are elegies. The lost psalms I carry inside me. No, but don't worry about that. Let's talk instead about this new bird I heard this morning. It too is another leftover from the October weather who has not flown south yet. I saw it high up in the tree, this small black and red bird who was signing the air with its voice. It rewrote the whole morning into mourning, its light notes so mapped with grief I looked around to see if its mate had fallen prey to some night time tom cat. Let us pray I say, I say it all the time, these days it seems it is all we have left. I look at the empty air between my two hands and can't seem to push them together. The other day my wife saw a white owl fly over her head, it hesitated in the air like a giant moth, before rising with one big flap and disappearing over the power station. She said she couldn't press the gas pedal to go she was so startled. But she did, she drove away. What I am trying to say is the miraculous is like that everywhere, but we cannot keep it, we must leave. There are children waiting to be fed. We have a pork roast to buy, some potatoes. Our bosses are waiting for us to punch in. But editor, dear editor, that great owl is still out there. He is still eyeing the ball field and the grass on the side of the ravines. He is dipping and swooping at night between the power lines of our backyards to eat the rodents. Can you hear the black bird's grieving psalms? Have you turned away from the blue light of your screen? Have you left your office to breathe in the scent of your sleeping child's hair?

Sincerely,

Dear Editor of Esteemed Northwest Review,

I am sorry I missed your deadline. I am a high school English teacher. I had piles of papers to grade. I am writing you from Washington State. I grew up on Puget Sound. My father was a fisherman. I am telling you because your guidelines say you like to hear something personal. I did not know that. My father was a good man. He taught me to tie a net. It was rare for a girl to learn how to fish out on the boats. But I loved most the mountains. Poetry is a kind of mountain we climb, I think sometimes. I doubt you grieved the absence of my submission. I know your deadline was last Thursday and I can't even imagine the thousands of submissions you received. The anxiety of it all! How do you even get yourself to look at the endless online que? An endless que of hope, though I hope you do not think of it that way, as then you might end up feeling guilty. Feeling guilty for being the killer of hope.

Did you hear about Hope, the girl who was taken while hiking in the Cascades? I often think of her, and her folks, her mother who appeared on TV. Or a thousand others? Another poster for the post office wall. How many parents who appear on TV begging for the return of their disappeared daughters, without a funeral, or a witness, their absence in the chair at the dinner table. Dear Editor, don't you think some things are beyond poetry? I can still see her walking to class, to sit in front of me, her ghostly abscess in the air—

Sincerely,

Dear Editor of Esteemed Journal Sponsor of Famous Contest,

It's not that I didn't want to enter your contest with the famous poet judging or that I didn't like the famous poet who I actually adore and own most of her books it's that I didn't think I had a chance to win or deserved to enter or have my words read by such an esteemed personage but when you kept sending me that Contest deadline with the COUNTDOWN a dozen times and then only THREE WEEKS, then it was TWO DAYS and each one addressed personally to me well I had to try so I sent you the 25 bucks I earned mopping floors for three hours and my six anonymous pages so six months later to see the announcement of the winners made and me not even notified, nothing by email, to just stumble upon the list, well…. Sorry, I got carried away, not on a stretcher sort of carried away, more like a kite on a wind carried away. Which is why I am really writing. Do you believe in miracles? Dear editor, I often think of poetry as a kind of miracle. You see, we always suspected my youngest daughter had cerebral palsy, her birth was difficult, her mother almost died, she looked dead. I can see her face. And the doctor's panic and the look on the nurses' faces and the blood, I'd never seen so much blood but, in the end, our daughter arrived. She laughed her first year and clung to us like a little monkey, she hated to be put down, but then she did the next year too, and she did not walk, she crawled and would not stand. The therapist from the state said she would probably never walk without a brace, until one day when she was nearly three she saw her sister running and simply stood up from the grass and fell forward and swung her hips despite what her therapist called her hip dysplasia and she ran a step, and fell, ran three steps and fell, flapping her arms like some flamboyant bird. Her heels never touching the ground. She is running still.

Dear Editor of Poetry Journals Named after Famous Cities,

I am writing to ask, have you ever eaten a cloud? You see my youngest daughter didn't use the toilet till she was after four years old. She'd shit in a diaper and didn't seem to mind. She refused to read till she was six though she spent hours flipping the pages of books and speaking out her made-up stories, but then what stories are not made up? Or her speech impediment, and the battery of tests on her brain. But today the sun was warm along the great lake. They call this weather Indian Summer, the red leaves and light. We were out on the back porch when our daughter reached up with her forked fingers as if to pluck the sky and turned and chewed, "I ate a cloud, dada, I ate a cloud!" Have you ever eaten a cloud, dear editor? You don't seem like the type, who has done this, with your Ivy degrees and serious statements on art. And what does a cloud taste like? Well, my daughter says, "Love. A cloud it tastes like love."

Dear Editor, Who Wrote Me "We Wish You Luck in Placing It with Another Outlet,"

I am writing you to thank you for your brilliant suggestion. The loans came through and now I invite you to the grand opening of POETRY OUTLET mall: the largest outlet for slightly damaged and remaindered poems in the world! Follow the large green neon sign at the exit off the interstate HALF-PRICED SONNETS and enter the hallowed doors painted like ivy walls where one can peruse an entire aisle of so discounted it's "almost" free verse, a turning carousel of sestinas or volumes and volumes of villanelles. Stanzas that stand on their own stands! Half price on all poems in accentual syllabic verse! Browse while sitting in the brown leather "professor" chairs. Amish buggies drive from miles around with their horse blinded carriages just to fill up on buckets and buckets of black suited and suspendered elegies: please do not stare at the veterans taking a knee or the weeping widows in aisle four. And the odes, oh the ODES how their syntax shines at the check-out counter—so many to choose from, odes to everything, even the things Neruda forgot: lady bugs, pantaloons and plastic duckies.

Self-scansion at check-out is available.

All Centos are BOGO!
All Centos are BOGO!

Come early, parking space is limited
due to our use of enjambed lines.

And don't forget to pay (attention to) the meter.

Dear Editor, I Did Not Go to AWP.

I did not board an airplane and travel to Florida and swoon and sashay through the book fair runway on what was my day off from working third shift helping to keep disabled people from dying, so Lisa and I splurged and went to an old school mom and pop diner for lunch and I had a great corn beef sandwich on black pumpernickel and she had a good chicken sandwich, and we had fries, and lemonade and black coffee it was all overpriced a bit but there was atonement in the air and all the old people who eat there for lunch probably every afternoon for decades left and no one else was there but us and it was quiet and she helped me go over some books I am judging for a contest, good books, too many good books, and we sat there in the empty diner reading poems back and forth, saying through words wrought by strangers into the room, and even the waitress disappeared, and there was just us, the snow falling in steady sheets outside, the last winter snow, hushed against the windows, and on the other side of the wall, at the bar, men were leaning over glasses of whiskey, whispering their lunch hour away. What I am trying to tell you is nothing more than this.

Dear Editor, Who Wrote "Though Your Poem Dublin Is Very Accomplished, and You Should Have No Trouble Placing It Elsewhere, but Not with Us."

I could go on and on about Joyce and The Dead and the martyrs of 1916, but really all that matters is what someone from North Dublin would do with your pissy tone? They'd throw a pint in your smug face. Not for us. Not in this neighborhood, not your kind need apply. I could go on like this, but there is a Dublin I carry in chest, one of ruby'd sessions and contraband guns, of women selling trinkets made in China along the River Liffey, one of centuries of blood and whiskey. One of harps and hunger. Hearth and rhyme. Quarantines and Guinness pies. I ask you who is us, across oceans sailing? Across ditches digging? The blackened faces of children in the factories and coal mines? The indentured Union dead? Who but us is belting out the Parting Glass, waiting to be served in Hell's Kitchen? Who but us is memorizing Yeats before leaving to drive a taxi through Dorchester? Who of us is waiting to open a letter from the Department of Historical Reparations? We crossed the equator. We laid the tracks, we fought your wars. You tell them to go home. But home we've made right here. It's in the blood. When I was born, I was born an expatriate from every country my ancestors spoke their beautiful vowels. In my heart, there is always a letter from them waiting to be written, waiting to be read.

Dear Editor Who Wrote, "We Have Decided Not to Select Any from This Batch. Best of Luck Finding Homes for Them."

1.
Why? Instead let them be gypsy poems. Let them caravan.

2.
Inside a tulip. Inside a hummingbird's ear? Rising on the Iowa horizon, a faraway silo. Inside a burnt spoon, inside a vein, inside the tight chord. Instead stopped breathing. Inside a coffin. Inside a sermon, a eulogy. Instead a drawer. Where I keep a box of bullets.

3.
A box of smoke.

4.
I wish you could have seen the red and yellow tailed sky stretching above the closed steel factory, as I drove home from working the night shift. The husk of the steel plant was a box of hope.

5.
What light is the moon like a eucharist in the mouth of the sky.

6.
The rusty cars lined up outside Flynn's tire shop. The entire city awakened to a lullaby named brother.

7.
A sudden door opens in the side of your chest. Does the light shine out, or in?

8.
My poems are ringing doorbells. My poems are asking for spare change.

9.
When I arrived home my daughter asked me what she should draw. A bird, I said. She said I don't know how to draw a bird. I said, then you should draw one. We only can do what we do and not what we don't.

10.

Poems should never have homes. Gypsy poems, poems driving RVs through the coal fields.

11.

My grandfather worked his entire life helping homeless teenagers not die. He would go out in the storms to look for kids to help bring to the shelter. There is a wind that reminds me of him.

12.

When I was 42, I was homeless for over a month. I lived in a motel. I had a room down a long driveway in the back. There lived a man who parked a Lincoln Town Car. He had the room two down from me. He didn't say much. He was over 60 years old, he'd sit and smoke cigarillos. I never saw him eat.

13.

Home is where the father rests his read. Home is where the mother bakes the bread.

14.

My mother says I should call home more. They are getting old. I haven't lived with them for decades and the house they live in I never did, but where they live is the place that fits the word.

15.

We are birds. We leave, we return. Or are we water? We never really leave. The faucet leaks.

16.

What language does not have the word home?

17.

The refrain we recall when we are most alone.

18.
To go home, like towards a country. Or a room. Or a door at the end of the hall?

19.
Where he was headed. Where he did not arrive.

20.
Odysseus in the blue light of the police cruiser.

21.
A long string of ghost children crossing these suburban streets

22.
A tavern, a bar, a motel where her childhood slept. A tenement at the edge of town.

22.
It was the kind of house that still had a string of cheap Christmas lights around the porch in June.

23.
The stream where we cast our lines. Where we never caught anything but broken bottles.

24.
What we leave in the rear-view mirror? Where our dead are buried?

25.
Refugee: a story that never can fully be told. Perhaps no more than an orange tree? What one remembers is no longer there, or was it ever?

26.
The fields at dusk long paved over. Only the street names are the same. The place where what has long been boarded up.

27.
What bright grief stands in a door blown open? Little by little it is
what we forget.

28.
What is home I ask my daughter?
My daughter lifts her colored pencils.
She draws four lines in blue.
She draws a yellow triangle. She makes a house.

No one lives here she says.
It is too small for the people
to fit inside it.

She draws her giant stick figures.

The children carry it, she says, like this:

And she carefully folds the drawing
and puts it in her pocket.

Dear Dead Editor, Who Never Published Me,

The critics fawned over your own often moving latter poems about your cancer, the ones I disliked because your earlier work was formally pedantic and made it easy to hate you, but then you got sick, and somehow you learned how to write, when faced with the white page of your own absence. But hate is not the right word. I mean do we ever hate anyone? Maybe that kid Jacob who beat us up in Junior High and took our lunch money or gave us a black eye? But even he we know probably got it good himself at home, with the belt buckle his drunken father swung. Children know the truth behind every cliché. We learn compassion not for ourselves but others. And now you are dead, the most common story of them all, and all the social media is declaiming you're good and great. But I suspect you were kind of an adulterous prick, seducing ingénues at summer workshops, and most of your work is metered ice, and only found some sense of compassion when you finally stared down that long hall waiting for the morphine drip. But empathy is not the sorrow of your own loss. And now you are dead, and the leaves are falling all along the great lake. And the steel plants are still husks like giant cicadas. Our fathers drink their retirement away at the American Legion. Our mothers wring their thick veined hands. These are lives you never saw or heard their stories sing. The word shift or shovel never appeared on your pages. For you it was all archaic urns and a language of porcelain shine. And to be dead is perhaps the final rejection, or is it acceptance? For seventeen years you never said Yes to me and I went on. We all go on as we must despite what small stamina we may claim. Who among us is not the outcast? And the years are measured by the trees we have planted, or the ones we cut down? If I lived in that wind-blown city, I would not attend your wake. I leave you to your sycophantic elegies. If to bad mouth no one I would argue against the mob it is the dead who often least deserve our praise.

Dear Editor, Who Solicited Me for the Cat Poems Anthology,

I am writing to tell you sadly I cannot participate in your anthology. I fear the anthology will be too full of sentimental pathos for my fragile self lately to bear. I find myself nearly weeping at the death of anything, even the moth that was trapped in the window or the sparrow that I saw eaten by the cat who then got hit by a car. What could I do with pages of dead cats, particularly since our oldest Cat Oreo (named after the cookie) is currently on her way out, after 21 years (human years). She has dementia and squats to pee continuously near the front door though (bless her heart) she still often remembers where the cat box is but never quite gets there, spraying her urine all over the wall for my father in law to step in in the dark and yell waking up the children. Soon she will travel to that place where cats go leaving an empty place on the couch or under the chair for us to look for her and call her name before we realize she is gone. You see it is better to step in cat piss than to miss it. This is something I think telling us about life and that often when we are getting pissed or pissed on or stepping in it, we should instead feel grateful and laugh for the stench of being alive. Let us get pissed drunk and laugh. For life is piss and shit and pain and going on.

And it is disappearance that I most fear. Like my friend Sarah's stray cat Clarence who adopted her one year. He just showed up in her backyard, this huge orange tabby and she fed him. Eventually he would let her stroke his neck. She'd take pictures of that cat and post them on social media, and I fell in love with him, wondered what Clarence was doing today. He had quite the following. And then one day he just never came back.

It is not death I fear dear Editor, it is not our cat disappearing into the dark I most fear, it is this disappearance without fanfare or goodbye, to simply be gone. Perhaps this is why we say cats have nine lives. They have lived with us for so many thousands of years. If they can come back, perhaps we will too.

Right now, our cat is purring at nothing, turning the air into honey. I had a cat once, a Russian blue cat, who would bring me birds it caught. It would come in in the morning and plop them down on the bed then sit there purring, letting me know what love is, and that not every death of a sparrow is despair.

27

Dear Editor, Who Made the Remarks about Not Wanting Walmart Poems,

The first thing I thought of was writing an Ode to an LOL, these little dolls that come in ovals that you open to find a different one (surprise!) that my six-year-old daughter is obsessed with and that my wife sneaks off to Walmart to find in the check-out line and bring them home and then of course the shouts of utter glee as she unwraps the crinkly cellophane and opens the puzzle-like oval to reveal what is hidden, what doll with a strange name like LIL Yin B B or LIL SHIMONE QUEEN or LIL MISS JIVE this mix of Afrocentric street speak and Chinese Pop combined into a world fusion of childhood rep. What my daughter does then with this piece of pop plasticine is what we could only hope: she imagines, she makes them talk and dance and sing, her tiny choreography and cabaret.

And such is the music we make now in this the 21st century, no different than that we first made with a carved piece of wood, these endless aisles of detritus made by workers and slaves, bought for a handful of shekels or wages earned by long shifts at night, like the ones I work taking care of people whose brains have been injured and their memories need a caretaker to get them through the day, and I think of D, who was once a foreman in a steel shop, calculating cuts on a CNC machine before an aneurism exploded and he had two strokes, and lost his job, and his woman, and his trailer down in a gully where every fall he would go and bow hunt turkey. Now he walks with a limp and one squinted eye, his left arm held up permanently curled and useless close to his chest, he slowly moves nearly hunchbacked with his cane. But D is all there, he can still do his math though his speech is stuttered and his eyes look crazed, he is still there trapped in that broken body, the one that when we go shopping causes strangers to pause and stare, with a tinge of fear, for what is different has always been the human way to suspect, and then to kill, or the way strangers stare at my autistic daughter throwing a fit in the check-out line, the looks and comments people make. This is how it begins. We other them. We say they are imperfect. We say look. The Spectacle of us: the damaged, the disabled, the different. There is always a them, amid the shining aisles of the things we worship we wander, the poor and broken, nodding at each other acknowledging defiantly there is also an us, and how could I ever forget the sight of those two loud white women riding in their electric wheelchair carts through the Walmart aisles, mother and daughter, hopelessly obese, not caring a damn what anyone thought, the mother hooked up to oxygen, looking at sales, as her black "grandbaby" no more than four years old, in pig tails and a tie-dyed dress, came running up to them with one of those damn LOL dolls my daughter loves, and then another, and another, and the grandmother and mother saying go find them honey bear, keep em coming, find them all, filling the front of their cart with what it takes to imagine something better—not elusive or remembered, but something right here, wheeling down the aisle, this exuberant process of accumulation, this ordinary awe—

Dear HR Person, Who Skeptically Asked Me to Explain What My Job at the Pool Hall Entailed,

The Vietnamese girls from the nail shop down the plaza gaggle into the pool hall trailing black feathers every Saturday after work are not really girls but women. But I am so old, women that young are still girls and my 18-year-old co-worker Jose who I ask, "Son, can you get me the broom," scolds, *Don't Son me.* What do I know? They arrive the five of them in black jeans and shirts, their informal uniform, the serious ones Duin and Sarah with their hair tied back with tiny loops and strings, can-sprayed-messy-updo to keep it out of their eyes. They lean like pros over the felt, blue mascara and tiny sequins on their cheeks catch the light as they play, all sporting nail extensions that somehow scimitar-curve without breaking or cutting the table. Gold hoop ear-rings dangling as they turn, and drink shots lined up five at the bar. Sarah is All-American princess: born in Buffalo, her father owns the Pho restaurant and the nail shops in town, she has a business degree from Penn State. Her father Mr. Tran plays billiards every Saturday. The wad of cash he'd bet I wouldn't bet against it. I seriously wondered whether he was a gangster. The other four Nailists all move back and forth between languages in the same sentence like my El Salvadoran friends, speaking a new dialect every immigrant learns reinventing English, piecing together what that means—like my great-grandmother from Hungary and her Yiddish slang *bubbeleh* for her son *Yussel.* The girls lean and sashay and clap like crazy when one makes a great shot. They are burning their tips. Two have black boyfriends. Duin wants to be a medical assistant. I have no idea how they know how to do nails. *Every Vietnamese girl can do nails,* Sarah teased. Her boyfriend Rashid has been coming here for years—I just thought maybe they met here. He goes to school for something with math, but he can't beat me at pool. Put that trigonometry to use I tell him. You mean geometry he says. He calls me *old head.* I bank the eight in. He shakes his dreads. The other boyfriend goes by Jaivon. He's always giving me a hard time about pulling up his pants—leaning over the table with his polka-dotted drawers showing—*I'm tired of this white motherfucker,* he hisses under his breath. Yeah, I say at least I have some sense not to walk around with my butt hanging out—what would your grandmother say? What would she say? Think of me as your grandmother. And this is my church. All I need is a church hat. Jaivon glares, *You ain't my grandmother.* Rashid deflects *Can you bake a sweet potato pie?* And they talk of pies as I walk away to clean a table. Sarah says, *we don't eat pie.* The girls are talking rapturous about something called *Che Bau Mau.* Duin cups her hands as if holding a mug, to show me it is a kind of dessert you drink. None of them know my father is black and old and kind, that his brother fought in Vietnam and wore those wounds for decades like a medal thrown in the Mekong sea, that he worked forty years as a social worker that my cousins cover a dozen nations, that still I carry my own ignorance out of the white lights—we cannot escape it. We are born into this infection. Jaivon carries a gun. But then who doesn't these days. I almost banned him a dozen times, ordering his girlfriend around. She swearing at him in Vietnamese, pushing him away. I honestly thought he was a piece of shit. Until one afternoon he showed up with his little light skinned brother. His brother was eleven. He was wearing ear muffs like the ones my daughter wears at school so the screeching of a pencil won't make her scream, with a stuttering and his fluttering of his autistic hands he asked, *May I play some pool?* And Jaivon said, *we normally go to the park, but it was raining, and he heard me talking about here and now he wants to play pool, what the heck—I didn't even know he knew what pool was!* He let his brother carry the balls to the table. His brother took them out one by one and placed them in order—Jaivon showed him the pattern to place them. It took his brother Ronny 5 minutes to arrange them. But Jaivon never rushed him. He taught him how to hold the cue, to lean and aim. Jaivon still clapped at every miss and said, *nice try little bro.* Or *you almost got that one.* When Ronny almost had a meltdown, he pulled a pop from his jacket. His girlfriend Duin showed up in jeans and no makeup. She started speaking to his brother Ronny in Vietnamese—and he spoke right back! He can speak Vietnamese? *He picks up things* Jaivon said. There was a tenderness and ease to them all we don't see in Jaivon and Duin on Friday nights when they are all outrage and posture in the eyes of their friends. Now every Saturday morning they hold mass. Now they breathe a kind of grace written between them like a choir humming through the church of this near empty pool hall, cleansing the air like the dialysis Jaivon's grandmother gets cleansing her blood. *They are cleansing her blood. Keeping her alive,* he said. He said his grandmother loves his girlfriend. He said she never questioned a thing, unlike his mother who doesn't accept her. They want to get married, but his job loading trucks at Walmart *pays crap. She's smart you know, but her English is bad, so everyone thinks she's dumb.* We are always cleansing the blood. The constant infection. You never know someone except for a few letters of their names they speak or the shape of their eyes or the names we mouth to erase one another till we learn the story. Once you learn the story you cannot claim innocence. Jaivon, I am sorry, I am always sorry these days. We are the infected we are getting better this early in a new and dangerous century, it is the same old epidemic since the first ship sailed. How we need to keep listening, to keep reaching: like Duin now stretching across the pool table, asking for the bridge to help her nail a long hard shot. And the girls—no the women: Vietnamese, American, slightly drunk and full of Vodka and light, they have their own power. They are clapping and shouting. Their hands glint and flutter. How can they shoot I wonder with such long and dazzlingly painted nails?

Dear Managing Editor of Esteemed Kentucky Poetry Journal, Who Wrote, "We Have Completed the Selections for Our Spring Issue, and the Editors Have Not Recommended Your Work for Publication. However,"

we can recommend a good bourbon to assuage your woes, or a good horse to bet on in the Derby, or a holler to sleep in, a place to hear your voice echo, a town inside a mountain and a mountain inside a town. Factories of baseball bats. We can recommend a bed of blue grass to lay one's head beneath the Big Dipper. Or is it the handle to a banjo playing "Orange Blossom Special" on a back porch facing the Norfolk Southern line? Can we recommend the mountain? Or go listen to Harlan County, you might never leave, find yourself lost among the Appalachian peaks? Bending to pick up a piece of coal the size of a working man's fist. Can we recommend a willow switch? Can you hear us in the Iron lungs and sorrow of the State Sanatorium for the feeble minded? Can you hear their ghosts on the sawgrass wind? Day lilies and Earl Scruggs playing in the mountain fog? We can recommend the strings that are strung across the chest, and the woeful sounds of the mourners beneath the lynching tree. These are the things we recommend. The ones that float like a butterfly and sting like a bee, in a shadow boxing Louisville gym, in a thirty-foot Lexington swish, in the whiskey and the chain gang's lament, we recommend the things we must never forget. Share croppers cooking up a mess of just caught catfish and kettled grits. We receive no compensation for recommending these to you. To pass the time. Buck shot and buck-naked boys diving into the creek's deep end. Mediums joining hands. To praise the Cutlass cutting hot across the pass at county's edge. Bootleggers and a pair of scissors, church ladies cutting free hair, gathered up in bags for the chemo patients. We can only offer something close to testify as we offer up rejection. Like a black-lung widow fumbling for an ashtray in a bar named Moonlight.

Dear Editor up All Night Sending Form Rejections,

How tedious the finger pressing the reply button through the night, and I know you must leave to work your third job soon, as a telemarketer taking calls all day, selling TV sponsored sorts of things. The best story from this work you told me about that NEVER BURN BARBECUE SET and how once slept deprived and delusional you offered to send FREE FIRE to this old man who had called but wouldn't confirm, yes, the set comes with free fire you declaimed. I will send you a box of free fire. Which is, I suspect, what you are looking for when scanning through the slush pile, the writing that will open on the page like a box of fire.

~

My friend Tony has insomnia, he works as a counselor and he told me his inability to sleep deepened his compassion. He said he learned what we are capable of simply from the lack of sleep or food, when he was young and poor and knew the gut fist feel of hunger's gnawing bone. For my job as a Medical Technician, I take care of a woman who is both always hungry and suffers endless insomnia. You see she has a brain injury where the thing in her brain that tells her she is full does not work. I could feed her 10 pancakes and soon after she would be asking me about lunch. She never sleeps at night. She once said, I could kill myself down in the hallway in my room and no one would know. Mostly, she says, when I ask her what is wrong, it is the loneliness. She is supposed to sleep at night. She misses her family who live hours away and her daughter she had to abandon after she was hurt. I am witness to so much so few of us think we could bear, but we do. Were you ever afraid? She calls her daughter every day on the phone. She texts like a teenage girl. Her speech often sounds slow, but she is, as we say in this job, all there, as much as any of us. She watches endless episodes of *Mom* and *Law & Order* and TV LAND. She talks to herself in a room with a kind of gibberish I can hear in tone is her speaking to her daughter before the accident, I visit between my third shift paperwork and cleaning. In the morning I will feed her and make sure she takes her meds. We will do some imaginative therapy where she describes, as best she can, her daughter getting ready for school. It puts her there across the miles. It brings her home. And really what little more is this life but the wish for a nap and a sandwich? A wish to smell your daughter's hair and watch her run in her yellow rain jacket to catch the bus. You can only hold so much air before the absence hurts the chest for anyone.

~

And you Dear Editor, leaning over a screen, pushing the same preset words with a long-callused finger, repeatedly sending out bad news, there is a kind of purgatory there, a kind of Sisyphus to this reply, watching the ball roll and then there are more hills to climb. Those nights you forgot why you even started to write.

To try to remember how hungry once you were, how you believed in art and what it could do: you are searching for fire out there in the dark. Or is it the dark itself you are waiting to find you, when you are hungry and sleepless for something you can't even name, the kind of dark we call to come to us, and wrap around our shoulders on cool autumn nights, when the city is not or never asleep.

Sincerely,

Dear Editor, with the Overly Kind Rejection Letter,

Thank you for telling me "the dead leaves"
are not good enough for The Sun.

Sincerely,

Dear Editor of Esteemed Bronx Literary Journal, Who Said My Poems Were Not "A Good Fit,"

Not a good fit, like a puzzle, a piece of a Borough pressed, as if they are more Westchester, Long Island, not even Queens. And of course, perhaps were not, as my understanding of the Bronx begins with Boogie Down. The Boogie, as from the French Bouguer, and before that Bulgares which referred to a group of "Bulgarian heretics," which means of course to Boogie to move "heretical," as one's booty bounces, and does not betray the beat. And as time passed of course as words become some sort of sexual and bouguer became bugger, as in sodomy (hence as in so many things English the ass is never far away) and then to the Devil (Bogie) which, of course, too leads us to all things dark, and the defined 19th century racist dichotomies of language: Darkies; the false linguistics that leads to lynchings until we arrive in Modernity and Africanized music gives us the *boogie woogie,* the birth of Jazz, spit in the eye of Jim Crow, and then decades (because this is sounding too much like school) take us to find the boom box blasting on the D train, kids popping their joints into graffiti, Kool Keith spinning two turn tables to symphonic city sounds, and at that time my great-grandmother Anna, in her 80s in the 80s, herself granddaughter of a freed slave, living up on the Grand Concourse, reads a poem by Langston Hughes to me and my cousins, and *night falls gently, dark like me* she sings, a pot of sweet potatoes brimming with brown sugar on the stove. Nothing is sweeter than Brown sugar, so the song sang. There is no need to say anything about apartheid or segregation or gentrification, just at the time I was 14 and visiting her and there were these Puerto Rican kids spinning on pieces of cardboard in the park down the block, adidas laced fat, the original (OG) Rock Steady Crew, who taught us the world is a dancefloor. Beneath the El three kids in Kangols are swapping rhymes. My cousins in Queens are writing furiously in notebooks. Fordham to Woodlawn. Van Cortlandt to Williamsburg to Morrisana: *The South South Bronx.* The epic Bronx. The Bronx of Dominican men playing three card Charlie and chess, the Bronx of old Italian bakers and Puerto Rican Madres cooking up pastels. The Bronx of Irish mothers saying the hail-marys at Saint Raymond's cathedral. The Bronx of Haitian kids conjugating mathematics on a 14th floor walkup, studying arpeggios and riffs. The Bronx of

Senegalese seamstresses singing as they sew. The Bronx of widows, martyred mothers, holding hard to their memories like pubs and parishes. My mother lived in the Castle Hill projects, graduated high school with her hair long past her hips, a cigarette slanted out of her lips. Once she cut class to catch the subway to the Village to hear a young Dylan. More than once she inhaled tear gas at an anti-war demonstration. She was the Bronx, not scared of police dogs or batons. The Bronx of body bags and so many who never came home. The Bronx of war dead and pianos. More men from the Bronx died in Vietnam than from any city in America. The Bronx of before wasted and then gentrified. The Bronx of Jews, Italians, Blacks. Nuyorican just arrived, working in the giant metal works. in the factories of pianos (at one time more pianos were manufactured in the Bronx than any place on the planet). This Bronx, of cascading energy, of musical notation, of the fallen New World risen. The Bronx of 14 languages in a five-block set. The Bronx of the El, weaving its steel tapestry passed tenements of families kneeling their heads to pray. If you were at that table, you would believe: take that father's hand: see how it fits: No one is shooting junk today. No one is nodding on the D train. The bakers are handing out free bread. And the Bronx river where two boys yesterday drowned is lined with nuns and mourners releasing a thousand floating paper cranes.

Dear Editors, Who Didn't Send Me Interesting Rejection Letters,

The ones whose imprint never even stayed, little more than the way a leaf palimpsest the sidewalk after being washed away by rain.

~

The same language we are told so often in this life: go away. And we do, and let the words leave us.

~

To you, I want to give you something, say, from the basement butcher shop, a leg of lamb, a bloody steak. You've done no damage, you left no mark, you let me escape, or was I recused?

~

And so, I hand you a glass moon of whiskey. A Ferris Wheel rising over the lake. The dark that rests after the wheat has been reaped. I send you what the bird feels, as the air first fills its wings. Even sparrows sing. Not only the rain can fill the emptiness of two palmed hands.

~

Soon they will ride in his blue Chevrolet and lay on towels down at the city park that runs along the lake, the sand full of bottle caps and cigarette butts, they won't care.

~

This isn't an analogy for adolescence, a story told to test, but a longing before loss.

~

To return to a moment before he left, and became an obituary I thumbed and paused, a feeling tight as a cord knotted and tied around my bicep.

~

I can see his girl strum her fingers through his hair, as in the distance giant tankers hunkered along the horizon line for the long haul to the open sea.

She is a while saying nothing. She feels selfish, an ache that pushes through the chest. This is nothing more than sad.

They never fought. It should have been enough to live.

~

And then she saw it rising: the great blue heron, flying right above their heads, over the edge of the shore, like an omen, of the end of anything we've been toughened by—

~

A sort of salvation shuddered—

when all the world we mourn returns inside you—

like the wind through a shawl of enormous summer trees—

Dear Editor, after Reading Your Journal, All I Can Ask, Where Are the Missing Words from My Life?

Where are the needles? The call-offs? The punch-ins? The pulse readers? Last night at work, I administered a new antibiotic for a participant suffering from a bad urinary tract infection: Ciprofloxacin aka Cipro, an antibiotic hard on the stomach lining and needs to be taken with a meal; dinner was taco casserole, a dish 2nd shift invented on a day 1st shift forgot to file food request forms for shopping funds, short on everything but tortillas, ground beef and "welfare" cheese. The med was for L who perseverates severely over any minor ailment, and lately had trouble ambulating due to the vertigo caused by the infection. He takes metformin for diabetes, lamotrigine for seizures, all my people take this and a PRN (as needed) meclizine for the dizziness. And all the usual for anxiety and high blood pressure, etc. Because most of L's problems are, he is just old, over 72 Italian-tough grew up in Little Italy on the west side. He fought in Vietnam as a marine and survived the battle of Hue, only to fall out of a PENELEC (the local electric company) truck nearly 20 feet, holding a soldering iron, while trying to fix a blown transformer. There are lights that grow out of the ground. They found him on the asphalt surrounded by snips of wires, fuses, heavy hammers, torquing wrenches, voltage testers, fish tapes and poles, from his tool box which fell too, miraculously missing him. He has survived decades with his brain injury caused by the accident. He is lucky he lived with thoughts, like a thousand tiny slips of paper all jumbled in the basket of his head. On his good days he likes to lie and tell everyone he was struck by lightning. He still has a full flock of oil black hair. When he loses his temper, he likes to say, "I'll plug your eye with my finger," and jabs his forefinger into staff's chest. We fill out IRs, incident reports, send to supervisors, write in clipped English. All you can do is laugh inside and be glad he still has it in him to get so angry over so little. What will we carry with us when we die? Any energy is good in one who has walked with death so long. His eyes are poor, so I put on my reading glasses and help him read his units of insulin and point to an unbruised spot of skin on his belly to insert the needle. What this job has taught me is what we believe we can bear is beyond what we can believe. At night he goes to bed

41

diapered in Depends, his Celtics quilt pulled close to his chin. We keep him on close checks. I quietly unlock his door and stand beside his bed in the blue light of Sports Center he leaves on as he sleeps: I stare every hour at his chest until I am sure he is still breathing.

*Dear Editor, I Am Writing to Ask You about the Last Time I Saw
You Standing outside of the Open-Air Market, Holding Those Heavy
Bags, You Looked Lost or Were You Listening?*

To that rare kind of soundlessness, like being suspended inside a
glass bubble as it is being blown, when you stand on a busy corner, in
a busy downtown, and everything suddenly stops: the women waiting
for the #6 bus, the old man at the crosswalk with his great sheep
dog, the boy who just a second ago was rapping the latest hit, takes a
breath. And then it bursts, the light changes, the traffic surges, and
the cacophonous orchestrations of living begin again. But for that
one tiny moment everything was still, and you felt the space between
you and others vanish, as if you could feel each separate inhale of all
those strangers, could feel the slightest turning of the earth.

Dear Editor, Who I Suspect Picks His Poems by Going Eenie Meanie Miney Mo,

And then catch what? When I was a kid in Toledo, Ohio in the 1970s we said tiger but we knew that was just a word that replaced the N word which none of us were allowed to say or said except a few of my black friends when their fathers weren't around and they were trying to sound tough or chummy with each other or said it to us, the other raggedy white kids who lived on those working class blocks, whose fathers worked in the factories of steel and auto parts and drank Schlitz beer at the UAW hall, but we knew enough even so small not to say it back, and Carolyn Robinson, this older black girl, kind and with a fierce sense of fairness, arbitrator of all arguments, the oldest kid in the alleyway by just a few years who, out of anyone in our lives may have raised us as much as our own mothers off to night school or to work as secretaries in the glass factories or at their jobs as nurses or teachers or selling perfume and stockings at Hudson's downtown. Carolyn whose own mother was a teacher at notoriously black and tough Scott High, when we picked sides to play chase or kick the can in a side alley where all our small fenced in yards faced, sticking the toes of our Keds and Converse dirty and with holes in a circle, five, six, seven, sometimes even nine of us, Franny and Tom, Anthony and Joey, Dianne and Debra, and every now and then Carolynn would say, Eenie Meanie Miney Mo, Catch a .. saying the N word and pause dramatically with a sly smile and we all looked at her surprised every time, the way it rolled so easily off her teeth, as if she was trying to define something for herself, or daring the world to say don't tell me what I can or cannot say, even if you can't, a word her mother Mrs. Robinson who spoke perfect Midwestern English and was legendary for reciting long memorized passages of King's speeches for her classes, might beat her with a broom handle for uttering, or was Carolyn telling us who were younger, white and brown and poor drenched in city grime and summer sweat, in our white string fringed Levi's cut-offs and t-shirts and too-short shorts and halter tops, who drank the rusty water from backyard faucets and hopped with one leap chain-link fences, that even something ignorant can't be what they tell you who you are, if every now and then you take it, coopt it and say it, and she'd give a little laugh to herself, before sides were chosen, before she ran faster than any of us, as if she has just said, Catch *this fire*, catch this star.

***Dear Editor, Who Wished Me Luck Placing Your Poems Elsewhere
(or Essay Tinged with Lyrics from 1980s Hits),***

And for some reason this song pops in my head called "Just Got
Lucky" by this band Jo Boxers from 1983, a strange sort of retro
sounding band that dressed in 1930s Little Rascals clothes and
bopped around on stage dancing, "I've been fooled by love so many
times/ I gave up on love and silly rhymes" which is rather ironic as
that was the year I lost my virginity on a bare mattress at a party on a
fourth floor tenement by the bus station downtown, when I passed
out drunk and this girl I'd go on to date mounted me, and the sound
of the song in my head echoes a deeper sorrow I can't place until
I look up the date it was released a month before my friend Garry
drowned in a swimming accident at the rock quarry where we'd dive
over the 20 foot ledges down in the clear water that carried us down,
carried us away from the oncoming future of graduation and looking
for work and all the unemployment of our city and the shoe mills
and GE with their long layoffs, and the nights we spent drinking
beers along the tracks along the river and talking about all we'd go
and do. How we bloomed in the blossom of the pouring rain. Is a
dream a lie that don't come true, Springsteen sang. We find those
dreams at bar stools in every town with a closed down mill along the
lake, in the melting ice of a whiskey glass. Or are they what we sing
when we've had too many, and that song comes spilling out over the
speakers, the one from when we were young, and our dead were still
living? We shout them out until our guts spill out upon the counter
and read our own entrails. What lost story do they tell?

The guilt that causes damage. It takes both hands to count our dead.
When was the last time I said I was going for milk and drove out
there to pour the liquor into the dirty sand along the lake, looked
out to the nation's dark horizon line?

I take a swig, I say their names. I drive home. I have a fast car. I
have something to prove. In the kitchen, I glance at the lunches you
have made with your labor swollen hands, the cheap lunch meat and
white bread sandwiches of our people. You've tucked our daughters
into bed.

45

But we did not die. We had no plan. We watched our friends drown, or OD, arms mapped with needle marks, or shot down for no reason in the dark. But we went on. We went on because we had to. We collected funeral cards we magnetted on the fridge.

We raised our daughters, we worked our extra shifts, we pulled our collars up against the cold Canadian wind.

And on hard nights, we raise our fists and curse outside the bars at the killing moon. I confess: There is a cello that constantly plays inside our chests, a dirge made of lost jobs, miscarriages and divorces, piles of bills unpaid, of not finding work and walking along the highway bridge, daring ourselves to jump. Sitting in the garage waiting for the gas. But we stumbled out coughing, didn't we? We raised the door.

After working second shift I come home, I put the key in the lock, I look in at our sleeping daughters. They are breathing, I walk down the hall to our room. I unloose my belt and let my jeans fall to the bedroom floor like bad decades passing in a blink.

And there O love, you are, already twitching in some bad dream in the red light of the alarm clock set for mourning.

I climb in beside you and pull you close, to ease the ghosts inside you: you wake and find my mouth.

O love, despite the odds and evidence, we are the lucky ones.

Our bodies driving fast into one another. We aren't anyone.

Dear Editor, Who Wished Me Luck Placing My Poems Elsewhere,

Forget the luck. Or the Japanese elm burning red like a slap to the face of the autumn air across the street from my friend David's flat. Forgot the tea kettle steaming on the stove, and the magnetted pictures of his children grown and his wife long gone on the fridge. Come and cross the tracks with me to elsewhere, over the 19th street tracks where the Norfolk Southern ran past tenements, right down the middle of the street for decades, spilling shiny orbs of coal for street kids. My friend David, now nearing 80 years old, lived on that block. He grew up with the rumble of the train, and the boot stomp of his father coming home from the steel plant to gather him in his arms, and his mother cooking up pierogi and Kluski for supper, and the lights they'd string across the front porch for Vigilia and the giant green spruce his father hauled from the empty car lot where they sold trees that Christmas, the one he was laid off, when everyone's father was laid off, and they gathered coal for the stove to keep warm, and they'd leap onto the passing train cars, to steal those black diamonds, to heat the house, that winter when they were hungry and his old man was out of work, and the snow fell in feet along the tracks, stopping the train and all the men climbing those cars to shovel out coal, and the sheriff and his men finally arriving. But all of that was decades ago. Most of these days David lives there, lost in the elsewhere that is not now, long after his father died, and David grew to marry the Irish girl down the block, and watch a son go off to war, two more marry and have children and join him at the GE plant, and watch their mother waste away from emphysema, and work his decades building diesel engines—engines bound for China and India, where millions traveled on the trains across vast states, migrating for work past the armies of children who squatted beside the tracks to gather coal to burn under the black of their mother's kettled brew. The 19th street line has long been closed, the tracks paved over. David's house is long torn down. I walk past listening to the hijab'd women laughing and speaking Arabic, bending to dig into the black dirt of a community garden The Sisters of Mercy built there, growing corn and tomatoes, cabbage and squash. What they grow they sell at the city's open-air market and share the profits. I watch them work when one of the women suddenly looks up as if she hears a train.

47

Epilogue:

Dear Editor, Today, I walked up the wooden steps and down the dim hallway and knocked, David answered the door, he knew my name. His caretaker had brushed his hair. He was dressed. All his buttons buttoned. He offered me tea. His left eye milky with cataract, he started to tell me something, but I saw already he was traveling elsewhere, staring out his kitchen window, somewhere far beyond the autumn Japanese elm still burning red.

Dear Kind Editor, Who Accepted My Essay: "Dear Editor, Who Wished Me Luck Placing My Poems Elsewhere," in 17 Hours. I Am So Happy, Because Where Is Elsewhere Anyways? Someplace Very Far Away? Or Most Likely Too Often Exactly Where I Live?

I am writing to thank you for your generous response and to ask, do you know where elsewhere is anyways? The other editor has really thrown me for a loop to loop. Any advice is greatly appreciated. You see I often have a problem with the present tense. My wife will be telling me something about what we need to do that day, to take our oldest daughter to the eye exam or to go to Sam's Club to buy one of those giant bags of dog food, you know the ones so large it is like trying to wheel an actual Saint Bernard, like the body of a pedophile murdered and bagged to the car on an episode of *Law & Order* we first watched together a decade ago, that she had completely remembered the ending wrong and I said we've seen so many episodes so many times perhaps our minds sort of collage them all together, mixing and matching segments, which brings me back to tell you what I was trying to say is sometimes, like anyone, I sometimes drift when she is speaking, my eyes out the window toward the lawn covered with yellow leaves, and I am thinking I have to rake those and asking myself if it is going to rain, and look higher at the gray slate of the lake sky, and then I am back but not fully, I am remembering something of when I was young, or maybe it is when she was younger, before she grew ill and lost all her teeth, or maybe I am remembering a memory she told me of once long ago how she and her boyfriend broke into the closed down paper to steal copper wiring to sell for dope, and there was a wild dog that lived in that factory, an abandoned pit pull they grew to know and would feed, leaving it plain double cheeseburgers from McDonalds which it would gulp down wrapper and all. We didn't think to unwrap them, she said, though we thought he wouldn't like condiments. Back then I often ask if she thought of what would become of her, or what she regrets, or grieves? You see I am not here even as I write this, and then I am back, back to her, and we are making a grocery list together.

There is a kind of list I make at work each night over and over with some of the men and women I take care of. We call it orienting.

When they wake up or seem to be about to have an outburst and motherfuck this and that we ask them, do you know who I am? Do you know where you live? Do you know why you are here? (the same kinds of questions the great Philosophers asked as they pondered being alive?) The greatest questions are often the simplest. But the answer we seek often is not, though I've come to ask myself more than once as I go through this life. But for B or A I must ask them to make sure they are not elsewhere. For when they travel, they will stay there. B will say, we are at college, or he will say home, or at mom's house. One time he asked a caregiver to tuck him in and said he was scared. This 45-year-old man had become 12. I tell him he is a time traveler. I remind him he is a man and watch him press the pieces to a puzzle of the planets or a kitten with a bow together, the way his mind so often tries to press and puts together the wrong pieces of his life into a jumble he cannot sort out with his hands. Where is elsewhere, I ask, Dear Editor? When our bodies are here, and our minds can look at the world right in the face and be somewhere else?

One day, B, being pissy and resistant to take his shower, I grew curt and said, listen you need to bathe. Where is your mind? And out of nowhere he turned to me and said, "I got my mind on my money and my money on my mind."

Dear Editor, what is the mind: how it turns and wheels, like a kite on a long string in a strong breeze, like the dragon tailed kite my autistic daughter and I fly along the lake. I watch her run with it. For once she is so present. Her small feet leaving tracks in the summer sand. I watch her reach that string high into the sky, the one we gaze on, for millennium, since we first stood over the savanna as night fell and one of us, the most present of us, pointed at those far and distant flames, and drew the lines between stars in the dirt with a stick to outline between the vast and empty elsewhere an animal or an archer or anything that was the shape of something familiar we could name.

Dear Editor, Whose Rejection Melted in My Hands like a Handful of Snow,

Sometimes what we have vanishes, we have it in our hands and it melts away like a handful of snow, leaving no memory. I remember the day decades ago I lost the letter from some editor in a snow storm. I was walking from the mailbox during a blizzard and the wind and the snow gusted and the letter I held blew away, erased into the white page of the air. I never figured out who that letter was from or what it said, I kept such poor records back then. This was when I lived in Syracuse, NY. I was married and had a small son. My marriage was bad, and I drank too much. Why was it bad? Who knows how loves starts to leave? At one point it feels nothing except like a warm summer day. Teenagers are skating along the river, and you are walking with a stroller or holding hands. You are making dinner together. The next thing you know there is a blizzard and everything in your chest is cold. You look down at your hands and what you held is nothing but air. What was it you carried like a chalice? Did you drink what it contained? You wake with a hangover in a room you barely recognize.

~

Sometimes what we write resembles us. Sometimes the face you see is no one you remember.

~

There is a day that what we have vanishes, we can't recall what it was we sent out into the world. You used to have a garden you planted, and you can't figure out what it was or the day you stopped planting and pruning. And sometimes it is just gone, like a memory you didn't know you once had.

~

On a day of snow, I received a rejection letter for an essay I didn't know I had sent out. It was to an editor I had once known decades ago, but we had grown apart for reasons I could not recall. I sent the essay, not one very good, in the mail to a journal that did not take online submissions. Years passed. When the rejection arrived, there was nothing in the self-addressed-stamped-envelope I had sent for a

51

reply. The editor had sent me back an empty envelope. But then I could smell the scent of something, and I know now he had sent me an envelope of his breath. Even decades later he was trying to save me.

Mouth to mouth, he was my friend back then. He tried to "give it to me straight," he tried to keep me from dying and I remembered how we grew apart, and my anger when I drank. The fractures and disappointments from my childhood I still carried, the violent streets that beat bruises across my chest.

Not everything that vanishes is bad.

Not everything we hold onto is good.

Is it really that simple?

~

On the first day it snowed, inexplicably I remembered the snow falling on the black hood of my ex-wife's cape. The snow melting into the wool, and the look of her face as she turned suddenly to look back at me. Where was she going, I wondered? Was I calling to her? What was it I was about to say?

~

Dear Editor, I ask you sometimes when we write is something close to confession? We write it down alone in the dark, with only the light of the keyboard, or the bare bulb lighting the dark ink of the page? We write to no one except our Gods? Hear me, we plead, each word we dare to stutter.

Or do we say it loud and clear?

We cut the stems off the flowers we bought ourselves and place them on the table. We wait until the room grows dark.

~

Dear Editor,

I must confess was a song by this 80s ska band, from when I was young and first in love. The song I thought was brilliant, this lilting upbeat dance track but when you listen to the lyrics you realize they are tragic: out like a light, another boy who has given up trying. I didn't understand it then, how it sang I have ruined three lives. The speaker of the song is singing after much time has passed. I didn't realize sometimes you have to let the decades pass before we can tell ourselves that one of the lives you ruined was your own.

I confess, I confess, I confess.

And then the saxophone solo.

Which is to say the saxophone augments or erases? Is it a form of snow, spiraling notes out that hollow what is in the chest?

Or a tunnel to drive through, a long drive on a dark road, after work when you pull into the drive, and the first snowflakes of late autumn are falling, covering the grass.

You go on.

We all go on.

Your ex-wife gets married and does well. She is a professor. She fell in love again. And so, did you.

The rain turns to snow erasing the world.

Sometimes what we have vanishes

we tell ourselves.

But it is all a fugue.

It leaves and returns, the way the rain does. You can't predict it. A certain smell like cut grass, or something baking on the stove,

or you find a shopping list in a handwriting not yours, folded carefully in a book, in a box.

And then it is gone. You do not give in to the melancholy or grief.

Because the flowers you bought yourself are there still on the table. And you remember when you realized, even in the dark, they were blooming.

Dear Editor, Who Said We Love Your Piece but Think It Could Be Improved by a Few Suggestions and Then Generously Gave Them and Said If You Decide to Revise It, We'd Love to See It Again,

And then when I sent it back revised, sent me a form rejection letter. I thought first, well maybe you have a lot of editors, or maybe the revision just never made it past the student readers so that is why it wasn't accepted, though I probably instead should have sent you the essay about the night I got so drunk at Scooter's bar with the East Side Biker gang after pool league, and nearly got stabbed by this big dude named Rudy for beating him at last pocket eightball a dozen times, and how this old white dude kept playing Willy Nelson's *Your Always On My Mind* over and over and singing to this bone-thin middle-aged blonde woman, who kept falling out of her orange halter top, named Lyndi at the bar, whose name I know because he'd shout out *Lynnnnddiiii, Lynnddddddiiii I luvvvvv you,* every five minutes or so, and how I snuck a double-shot of Makers Mark out to the parking lot where I borrowed a Newport off this black dude named Maurice (right? Like Maurice Lucas) and we started talking about the 1979 NBA Championships and how both of us had that poster of Dr. J rising from the foul line to dunk and then we sang the Converse commercial, *hey Dr. J where'd you get those moves, are you wearing magic shoes?* It started to rain there a block from Parade Street and I was outside in the parking lot on that late summer city night, drinking whiskey cut with rain water, when these sirens blistered by blistered the air they were driving so fast, headed toward some other dive where someone was knifed or shot, or maybe they just really needed to make it to Mighty Fine Donuts to get a cruller and coffee before it closed, though it never closes, open 24 hours, they make the donuts right there! Best damn donuts I ever had. My friend Sal used to work there till he had an accident with a pipe, and it bonked him on the head, and now he's on the disability, living off that government check. I meet him there for coffee and I read the paper to him as his eyes get blurry and give him headaches, I read to him about the shootings and the weather, and sometimes the obituaries for anyone we know and the want ads for work he might be able to do, though we both know he can't. He believes every conspiracy theory and he's been listening too much to this Neo-Nazi named Hank he met at AA. Now he sits at home and feels sorry for himself and scans the internet for

evidence he's been screwed by anyone with a dark face and the Jews. But I digress. It was the night I got drunk and wandered down to Mighty Fine to get a donut and sober up, and sat there at the counter across from two detectives I made, dunking a chocolate glazed into black coffee and for some reason they really pissed me off, they were just laughing and chatting and talking about that night's Steelers game, so I kept repeating the names Trayvon Martin, Eric Garner, Tanisha Anderson, softly like a chant, like a mantra, and sipping my coffee, because I felt brave I felt angry and brave and I was white and old and I thought really who gives a fuck, it has to stop, might as well be here, because those detectives didn't even look up until on the way out one went to the cash register and turned and pointed at me and said, I'll pay for his, and then walked over and put a hand on my shoulder and gripped it hard and I thought I was done, I kept my head down, but instead of pulling out the cuffs he said, "A thousand, thousand sighs to save,
For you have but mistook me all this while:
I live with bread like you."

There are cities beneath us and inside us, cities we live inside and ones we walk to read. We turn a street and everything and us then changes, and all we thought we knew disappears as we walk on steady legs, suddenly sober past bodegas and closed down pharmacies, past tenements where music spirals down in curls like the dark curls of a woman sashaying uphill, humming in headphones, who leaves the air smelling of patchouli, and you leaf the wreathes you've carried, for a moment you lay them down. What can you do but "Cover your heads and mock not flesh and
　　　blood
With solemn reverence: throw away respect,
Tradition, form and ceremonious duty." No, instead you bow your head, right there on the boulevard, like someone kneeling.

Sincerely,

Dear Editor, Who Never Got Back to Me,

My youngest daughter, all her front teeth missing, was asked for Children's Grief Awareness Week, "What would you do if a friend lost someone?" They had given her a drawing of a purple butterfly to put her answer. On its wing in tiny awkward letters she wrote "I would help her find them."

There my poems were in the online que, four months, then six months, and now it has been too many and so I do think they are lost in some sense, eyes turned down, walking past us on the street, or at the factory, in the waiting room at the ER,

lost like the men I cared for at the residential house, this young man Nick, huge and gangly, over six feet tall, non-verbal, autistic, who for no reason would just start to shriek so loud and unexpected he would even make the house manager who had worked with him for years jump out of his seat.

Once he looked right past me and then smashed his head against the table. Where did he go? What could we say? What were our voices we threw him every hour to bring him back? He bent his head over the quiet tapping of his fingers and suddenly calmed.

He was tapping out a sound, a music, to the hum of the refrigerator. He slowly ate his cereal, he signed for more. I gave it to him. I gave him what he asked for.

For so much of being lost is not just being found, but not making our way home to walk in the door where we feel safe. But there is always time passing us by. We are drowning in its river. We call the Bureau of Milk Cartons. Who is that face we do not recognize?

Somewhere there is official documentation we are not dead, nor *Lost* like in that confusing television series I could never figure out, I thought the writers made it up as they went along.

I guess we all make it up as we go along, I feel that way so much as a father, watching my children stop crawling, or lose a tooth, or gain a friend, or lose that wanting to be held all night or come running when they fall or bruise. How much do we lose along the way?

Sincerely,

Dear Editor, Who Said Please No Third-Rate Raymond Carver Imitations,

I tend to drive into things, my vision poor at night, a little worse
each year the older I get. Last night I drove through snow slushed
streets of November on the way to pool league. I was rushing a bit
late as I stayed to listen to a long funny meandering story my six-year-
old daughter told about her LOL dolls but left before she finished,
and she started to scream. I sped through the city past the closed
pawnshops and the social clubs full of drunks. I turned too soon
into the parking lot at the VFW and smashed my wheel into the curb
blowing out my front tire. I thought to myself, I am so fucked. This
was my fourth minor accident. I pulled up the icy side drive and left
my car under a streetlight. I played poorly for three games before
I could get the accident out of my head and beat my man in the
fourth. My teammates kept me laughing and played great and we
pulled out the match, hitting the right shots and playing the right
safes, and getting a little bit lucky along the way. Let us praise the
roll that goes a little too long when we need it. Shawn blew $20
on the slots and all of them were buying and selling cues on their
phones during the match. The banter these days both in the house
and in that space electronic at the same time, even for grown men.
There was a haze of gauzy smoke from Camels and Newports that
hung over the tables and felt. There was already a plastic Christmas
tree and tinsel everywhere. The old veterans and working men and
women sat at the bar counter drinking their double-shots of Maker's
Mark and those big fruity drinks whose name I never know but could
all be named Desire or Divorce. They'll put you on your ass, and
the players had these aluminum buckets on their tables filled with
Pabst on ice that were on special. The team from the black VFW
on the East Side was there, old Boo now nearing 80 years old and
still leaning his shaking arm over the rail's edge made some nice
cut shots. He did two tours in Vietnam. He was on the same team
as Larry who isn't very good, but his son Markus was a Juniors pool
star. Markus is all grown with dreaded hair and 40 extra-married-
well-fed pounds. He works as a barber after dropping out of Penn
State. He said *I just fell in love with cutting hair.* He still has his stroke.
He drew the ball the length of the table to get out on the eight. We
are all now old enough to witness our sons and daughters play beside

their fathers. We have become our fathers moving slow around the table. All the wives, good players themselves who shoot on Tuesdays, drank until they were half-lidded. They teased their husbands every miss and poured $10 bills like water into the no-one-ever-wins slot machine. No one was talking politics or of the dead. No one was shot this week we know. No one OD'd. No one hit the daily. The snow was falling outside in big lumpy flakes. At the end of the match, no one didn't shake hands, or high fived or even hugged those hard half hugs that men give, glad to see you and the small things we say of good luck with that new contracting job, or your daughter's basketball game, or that court case. Outside the parking lot emptied and all that was left was the night. I leaned over my trunk. I had one of those little spare donuts and was able to get it changed with help from my buddy Daren who did not drive away. I am sure he really wanted to get home to his wife and kids. He works as a postal worker and must get up in the AM but stayed to help me without asking. He had all the necessary tools, including a compressor to fill my flat spare, that looks like a toy; it always makes me think of the tires on the red wagon I'd pull my son with along the bay. He'd sit in the back pointing at everything and naming it "puppy" or "bird." Perhaps every cloud was a bird? Perhaps the dark was a kind of bird that wrapped us in its wings? My son is all grown now, works in computers, calls rarely. He might as well live on a cloud. Where did it all go? The divorce between his mother and me? Decades disappear like mortgage payments. The snow keeps falling in giant white flakes that stick like spit. The endless layoffs and jobs, a second marriage, illness, hospital stays, operations, two daughters who hit each other with sticks and scream and laugh across the lawn's dead grass. We get to work, we change the flat, we drive away slowly through the slush to those we love, long asleep. The axle makes a noise as I turn. Because still the noise it reaches in. What things we smashed we thought we fixed along the way when we weren't paying attention?

60

Dear Editor, Who Said My Poems Were Almost,

My people drink too much. I'm driving and there's my friend Tim headed to the corner store to buy a 12 pack at noon. I stop, I pick him up. He tells a story about his friend Donny fighting cancer. How he could have been a famous rock singer. He says he's going to drink the afternoon away. I let him out as a cop watches us. My people all are elegies. We are on 16th street, where people often stop on corners to buy meth or junk or coerce with prostitutes. There used to be a great old man bar across the street where old men drank slow from opening at 10 AM to close. But then they all died. The bar closed. My wife is often drunk. She hides bottles of Vodka in our daughter's closet. She lies to my face when I ask if she's been drinking. She lies so much I begin to doubt myself and think maybe I've gotten paranoid. Then she feels guilty and confesses and gets clean for a while. My friends close bars like the rich close factories. With each one, a little piece of my people dies. We drink away our mortgage payments and our divorces. We drink for joy after working 10-hour shifts. We drink to forget our foremen. We drink with our foremen to forget our foremen! We drink in giant sippy cups we sip when we drive. Our mothers and our daughters drink. Our sons are doing time for getting caught drinking and then driving into someone's lawn. We drink after crashing the backhoe. There are a thousand bars with our names of our dead scrawled into the counter. We sit at the bar and talk about how so and so was almost famous. The bartender wipes the clouds from the counter and my people lean over to see their blurry faces. My people count out change from change purses to buy 50 cent drafts. My people drink the light from clouds, they drink the dust from fireworks. We drink the dark. We drink well-scrubbed floors. We drink broken axles and Free Enterprise. We spoon honey into our whiskey. We spoon whiskey into our wine. We put spent shotgun shells on our fingers. We drink cesarean scars. There are accordions in our chests we press as we rise in camo hoods. Our hands are covered with engine grease. Someone lights a match, burns a letter denying benefits, the ashes plume into the air like black butterflies above the bar. And what do we do when the rent is due? When we don't have anything left to pawn? We breathe into an empty shot glass. We tell that same story about who could have been if only. Sentences float from our mouths like meth. A dirge of apparitions that were never. My people's almost odes.

Dear Editor, Who Apologized for Taking Six Months to Reject My Poems and Said They Came Close,

I woke this morning at 5:26 AM to the sound of my wife opening a bottle of Chianti. I said to her, "The Breakfast of champions!" She said she was up to six hours between drinks. She's trying to quit again. The doctors have told her she will die soon if she doesn't. She's cutting down with wine. The house is littered with secret pints of Vodka, hidden in drawers and closets. She takes a slug to get through each room. I do not know about the garage. She lies when she is at her worst. She slurs and insists she's sober. Sometimes the girls find the bottles and bring them to me. Some days they are enough to drive anyone to drink. I do not judge her. But I would really like her to stay around, I tell her. Sometimes the way she holds her head she looks like she is a painting by Vermeer. There is a darkness she wears like wool. My wife persists despite her own wreckage, the years of illness and hospital visits. And what about you my friend asks at work, do you persist? I don't have time not to I say, we have the girls. The hardest part is I have to imagine her not being here even though she still is. I must prepare myself to go on. There is something ghostly to her absence. Perhaps the damage to myself is unseen. I am not angry. I am like a bottle that has been smashed and pieced back together with apologies. My bones are leaking light. I can feel beneath my skin are shiny fractures. When I walk outside, the wind blows right through me and you can hear my body whistling the saddest song.

Dear Editor, Who Returned My Poems and Said They Weren't Taking Submissions but Didn't Tell Me When to Submit,

To whom or what do we submit anyways? I find a bottle my wife had hidden. There is no shame in this. I imagine her sneaking into my daughter's room to take a swig, those mornings the girls are screaming and punching each other. My oldest daughter has Asperger's and can throw a fit that has no end. Though she has gotten better at controlling them as the years have passed. I talk to her about the anxiety, the roll of sound and voices that push her to thrash herself around the floor. I tell her I used to have it bad, so much they gave me tiny pills to help. I said it made the voices quiet and go further and further away. Then I tell her I learned how to push them away by myself. I told her they aren't real. I told her only this is real, and I rubbed the top of her head. I told her the things we tell ourselves often aren't real. I told her start to tell yourself some things good. She says, ok. She says she deserves a time out. She walks away and immediately begins to torment her sister, telling her she eats poop. But an hour later she freaks when she cannot finish a math problem and begins to howl, but only for a moment. And I think perhaps she is starting to listen, she is starting to realize this world is full enough of things to hurt us but the one who can hurt us the most are ourselves. Her mother says no when I ask her if she is drunk. The bottle I found in one of her hiding places is missing. She says she had to go to the store to buy snacks for the girls. She must go somewhere to get what she needs.

~

I work with a man with a brain injury who suffers from anxiety. P is small and overweight and has wounds on his face from where he picks himself. The first time I saw him have an attack, I told him his laundry he had left in the laundry room I had folded but put into another man's room. Both wear lots of camo. He rolled his eyes then let loose a litany of undirected profanities, motherfucking this and that, he was so angry. Later a staff told me this happened before, and his clothes had gotten mixed up. I wondered if P was picturing his clothes mixed up with the other mans. He did not think how his name was written on every tag. He was picturing not having any clothes. He was thinking too, how do they not know my clothes?

He felt invisible. He walked outside away from me cursing and lit a cigarette. He had learned to walk away. The wave passed. Days later I sat with him on the smoking benches outside and told him, I am proud of you. We spoke of how he was angry at me. I said but you walked away, that is a good way to at first handle it. He said yes, I need to let that big wave in my head come crashing down, and he lifted both his hands high over his head then let them fall. Then I can become calm. He took a drag on his Newport, watched the cloud of smoke hang in the autumn air. But I was mad at you for a long time, he said. That will pass I said, that is the residual anger in your muscles. it can last long. The trick next is to learn how to walk away in your head, you are getting better. I want to get better he said, I don't want to be that wacked-out dude with my hoodie pulled over my face telling everyone to get the fuck away. He pulled his sweatshirt hood right around his head and scrunched his mouth and eyes up and crossed his arms. He looked like an angry injured elf, I start to laugh so hard I fell sideways on the bench. He paused and asked, why are you laughing. I said, that is funny, didn't you know how funny you can be? He beamed, I didn't know. I said, now that is something to work on. Let yourself he open like that. Your physical gestures are magnificent. He looked at me as if I was completely daft. Then said, my whole life I have always feared people laughing at me.

~

Who isn't? There is nothing close to shame. But then we learn how absurd it all is anyways. My wife is doing a load of our youngest daughter's laundry. She must be the most functional drunk on planet Earth. She folds our daughter's tiny shirts so perfect, each one lined exactly on the edges. She doesn't hear me in the hall. I watch her stand and look at the piles of perfectly folded clothes. She doesn't move, admiring her work. She works slow and precise. She told me once she is always scared of failing. Who of us doesn't constantly fail? But the miraculous is all around.

Outside the light itself is failing, the grey sky of November. I submit this anecdote as evidence. The early dark is on its way. Our daughters are outside kicking leaves, when the oldest pushes the youngest down taunting her. She grabs her big sister's legs and pulls her on top and they begin to roll and punch. They are both howling, rolling and wrestling, saying eat this leaf, eat this leaf like poop, shoving leaves into each other's mouths, pushing each other's face into the cold dead grass, calling for help that never comes, I let them go, I let them fight and learn what a struggle love is, and then they are still, worn out exhausted, laying their arms out wide, side by side, staring up at the dark that settles over them like a blanket of blown leaves. And then they begin to rise, just barely off the ground. They hover there, like two oak leaves held for a moment by the rising wind.

***Dear Editors Frantically Flushing out the Slush Pile before Christmas
Break,***

I received 7 rejection letters in the last 8 hours, which means for nearly
every hour I was at work last night, doing room checks, making sure no
one died, checking blood glucose, hanging Christmas stockings with
the poorly scrawled names of the men and women we watch over in a
long and jagged string, sweeping up rock salt and the dust of the day,
an editor was reading my work and thought well this isn't quite what
we are looking for, looked for, not for us, these words, are not, are not
including one from the literary journal Field who I had informed in
my cover letter as usual was the first place I ever sent poems 30 years
ago. I had of course dutifully periodically submitted since then every
year sending a stamped-self-addressed-envelope off to Oberlin and
then an electronic file. Years ago, I taught as a poet in the schools in
the Oberlin public schools and across Ohio. I remember driving the
narrow routes through the snow-covered fields and traveling south
from I-80 past single school houses with Amish children walking to
class on the side of the roads that cut through grand and endless
rows of wheat and corn. This is not a poem. There are no words in
the snow blowing off the interstate today, or in the small blue hats
of Amish girls wear as they wait for their black suspendered bearded
fathers, or in the cheese curding, or in the milk cows braying against
the wind blowing south off Lake Erie, there is nothing for me to
say about the lake freezing, or Franz Wright who wrote of the snow
blowing like dead bees. Or was it burning? Or his father who taught
for years at Oberlin, long before I started writing poems and the boys
of Ohio galloping desperately into one another one last weekend of
autumn, here on the rim of winter, on the eastern rim of Ohio, and
the names of the dead painted on the sides of barns and Silos, or
the skyline of Cleveland rising in the distance, with its archipelago
of lights you can trace from space. Electricity that carried my poems
one last time to Oberlin and Field now is going to cease publication,
so I submitted, and I actually received a human response for the
first time in about 20 years: "Thanks for your good words. Sorry we
haven't been more receptive.

Sincerely,

DY"

Dear Editor, Who Said My Work Was Too Narrative for Their Journal,

I've been telling a lot of stories lately because of where I live in a story. We are stories. My friend Jose Rosario who was shot dead on his back porch is a story. I've been in a down place for longer than I can remember lately, mapping my failures in these little essays I've been writing like rungs in a ladder I am hoping to climb, though out of what or toward where I'm not sure.

~

"Dear Dead with beauty on them as they lie." Perhaps everything I write are letters to my dead?

~

Jose was only 18 years old. I knew Jose from the pool hall where I worked the counter. He came up through our Juniors league. I can still see him when he was small, with his flattened down Afro, trying to hold his cue, balancing it on the table's edge, as his coach taught him how to stand correctly, feet shoulder apart, chin down. I can still remember witnessing Jose's joy as he started to consistently sink balls, his right arm moving in a fulcrum. He was an emotional player. He felt the losses but always shook the hand of his opponent. As years passed and he grew precise, running a rack of eightball from the break regularly, I saw him lose on purpose to many a younger weaker player. He'd turn to me at the desk and shrug and wink. He'd tell them what they did well and wrong in such a gentle way. He was a good teacher. He was a good kid. After he turned 16, we worked with us at the pool hall. He wiped the tables, he ran the register. He grew tall and wiry, his limbs stayed thin as cues. But I witnessed his body learn how to stand firm against gravity, the weight that presses us down in this world.

Someone blew Jose away and some of my other friends are searching for who did it. People are asking questions. There is so little word on the street. What do the police care? There is a story that needs to be told here, about Jose, about violence, about guns. About this nation we live in that doesn't acknowledge our children are at war.

Or is it more a story about the flowers I saw on the news sitting on the kitchen table as his mother looked at the camera and called for someone to come forward?

The police don't care about a dead Puerto Rican kid.

Dear Editor, what about that story? Can you tell me that story?

~

Hélène Cixous described words as steps on the ladders of writing. I don't know French and always wondered why she used the word "step" and not "rung."

~

Often, I feel wrung out by my work, like laundry in the hands of an old woman at the end of the day. I feel wrung out from the losses. The last red maple leaves of autumn are buried under the snow.

~

Last night the nuns held a vigil for Jose in front of his house. Friends and family stood in the dark of late November holding candles.

I drove by slowly. I could not stay. I had worked a double and I was too tired. I had to buy groceries and make dinner as my wife was at her rehab appointment. All of this was true. But I did not stop because the flames of those candles burned my chest. I saw Jose's mother there, head bent and praying.

How much of what defines us in this world is what we bear to witness?

~

Whoever shot Jose walked in his back door. The door was open. He turned toward the door when he heard it, and someone shot him and ran into the East Side night. No one can say more than that or anything. His friend from his pool team tells me she cannot sleep. She just had a baby and the child cries all night. She said she can't stop thinking that Jose will not know her daughter. She talks to me with words like tragedy and justice. There are no words we can truly say. We use the words we are given.

At the end of my shift I always am sure that the mop I use to mop the building is well washed in the sink and wrung out. I hang it to dry. Something about it dripping in the dark tells me my labor is done, but really it means my work has just begun. I must get my people up then, to give them meds. To help them dress. To feed them.

I put the bowels of oatmeal before my people. We bend our heads over the bowel we have been given.

~

I punch the clock. I drive away into the dark. I drive past the house of my dead friend. Jose's mother must go on. His brother must go on. Someone said the shooter was looking for Jose's brother. They shot Jose by accident, looking for his brother. No one knows what the story is? We are all just rumors. The police act like they are looking for no one. Who cares about a dead Puerto Rican kid?

Sometimes after work I am so tired from hearing the curses and outbursts of the men and women I take care of—I sit in the parking lot for a long time, letting the car run, listening to some lame pop song. I've seen the other workers do this too. As if we are waiting for something to arrive, or to let go, so we can pass back into the normal world.

~

Perhaps these words are little more than a map of all my failures? Someone opened the back door to Jose's house and walked in.

~

I am a cartographer of the losses in my life? There is a story in the paper that says my friend was murdered.

Why must words become a ladder? Or a map? Why can't a word be a word, something that and only by itself can open the body? And becomes breath?

69

Was Marjorie Waldrop the one who wrote that "the word" becomes "breath" that "opens the body?"

~

Marjorie, what would you say to the fact that a bullet is what opens the body?

~

The word always wants to shift to become something more than a word.

But in this life the words I use are little more than words.

Jose used to squint as he leaned over his cue. He squinted one eye so he could measure the shot, then opened it and let the cue ball fly.

I say the words to the people I take care of. Bad days I realize they are little more than directives masked as questions. Did you do your laundry? Do you feel ok? Did you make your bed? But the best days our words become invitations: Do you want to fold your laundry together? Do you want to take a walk to the road? Do you want to play a game of rummy?

Can you see the shot, his coach would ask Jose? Can you feel it? Can you become one with the cue?

At work the directives we give our people are called cues.

My friend is dead. How much of our lives do we spend just hoping someone will invite us to do anything? We are waiting for the cue that means, come in. We do not know what will happen when we open the door.

So, I Submitted My Epistolary-Essay "Dear Editor, Who Wished Me Luck Placing Your Poems Elsewhere" for Submission and It Was Form Letter Rejected. This Is What the Last Line of Their Rejection Said: "We Wish You the Best of Luck Placing This Elsewhere."

I really appreciate you adding "best" because I sure could use "the best" of anything in my life. I've never made those best of anything lists and as years passed, I grew to not even notice them. They reminded me too much of high school, prom king and queens, the social hierarchies of the north side kids, the rich kids from the upper middle-class houses along the fairytale named subdivisions with titles like Sherwood, or Glenbrook, or Lawndale, or any sort of Forest, Park, Hills, Waters, Crown-point, Estates or even Plantation. All the red lined white-faced places without sidewalks. Where the odds are in your favor

not to meet someone who isn't white and speaks uninflected English riding the subway and swaying in a car of fifteen languages, or on the bus, and giving your seat to the old hijab'd woman from Iraq or Bosnia or Alabama, or an ex-army vet asking you for change, or the people who live in flats and rooms, which are rented from landlords who live out on the edge of town, and send their kids to anti-gay camps, and sing thanks for their affluence to their white-faced God. Rooms for rent along the ex factoried streets named by number, and someone is hitting the radiator with a spoon to get it to work. What are the odds no one has lead poisoning, or the water isn't tainted, or they won't be mugged in the dark hallway? To live without the fear of something shattering. What is holy is the light

that stretches over tenement roofs in winter, and the sound of children shouting in Spanish, Arabic, English as they play in the slushy streets. No one was shot today. No one hit the lottery. What are the odds for any of them that grace these crowded kitchens, pots bubbling on the blue ring of fire, parents cooking after working double shifts, Baba dozing in the tattered brown recliner, uncles arguing over poker and soccer, and somewhere the baby is crying, where a dark-eyed teenage girl in the steamed kitchen window draws a heart with her finger, places it to her mouth as if to say hush as she looks down at the street, where someone is waiting for her to sneak out, the snow falling quiet as moths.

71

Dear Good Reads Reviewer, Who Gave My Book One Star,

I take that one star and make it into a star on a piece of wide lined paper in first grade the year my dog was shot beside me for peeing on the old man's lawn, the year the girls next door took me down the basement stairs and beat me with a stick and called me names. It was a room dusted with cruelties. Tonia was the oldest one. She had an exceedingly pathological sensibility she inflicted on the younger children on my block. She was tall for twelve, near six feet tall and willow thin. She beat us all with a stick she made us choose. She made us call her mother. She made us take off our pants. It is hard to tell this story even now. There is no loom to weave the threads of what she did to us to make it any easier. But her indiscriminate cruelty made it easier to survive. One day she grabbed my friend and for reasons I cannot say I picked up a crushed aluminum can and flung it like a throwing star at her head. I'd had enough. I was six years old. It hit her perfect and she fell to her knees as if praying. There is no damage I can spell of what she did to me that day. She hit me where the bruises did not show. I did not tell. But as her blows fell, the blood from the cut on her face did not stop bleeding, it kept having to pause to wipe the blood from her eye. Her sister whose name I can't remember, though I've tried, was a follower who died of an overdose I heard before she reached adulthood. Her uncle raped her for years. I can't even picture his face. He drove some sort of fast car. He had the kind of dog that could hurt you. He beat it with his hands. Those who hurt us sometimes are hurt by others even more. All we can do to escape is to stare into the tiny piece of starlight in our heads like a lamp someone is holding in the distance through the dark.

I saw Tonia when I was a grown man, she wore dangling star earrings. I recognized her at the bar up on Detroit Ave. She did not know who I was. She was drinking Vodka and talking to a man who looked like he would do her hard time, a light-skinned man with a jagged scar like lightning across his cheek. I was visiting my childhood friends, all out of work. The part factories closed along the lake that decade, the smartest one of us was washing dishes at the mall for minimum wage. The whole neighborhood was whispering toward winter. He kept squeezing a Kleenex he kept in his hand.

We let go the violence of the young. But there was the time my wife saw that girl who tormented her throughout elementary school, who showed up to watch the Monday night Steelers game with her loud suburban coeds at the bar she did not know we claimed as ours, who recognized my wife as if they had been close, who put her arm around my wife before we were married, long ago, and I saw my wife's face darken, I watched waiting for Tiresias to bring her back. But he did not cross the river. She open palmed that woman so hard in the face we watched her fall to the ground knocked from this world into the next. I thought she was dead. Her friends lifted her across the beer spilled floor and carried her out. The cruelty of children is not what we need to take with us into this world. Leave it there down in the darkness. Dear reader, I take that one star and make it gold and foiled. I keep that star inside my chest. I take that star and make it the Star of David for my grandfather, the son of Jewish immigrants, who grew speaking Yiddish in Yonkers, NY, my grandfather who worked years as a social worker helping kids get clean and off the street. The junkies with their heads nodding like lilies. Who wears the wounds on their feet and the darkest shade of lipstick? Who is heating a spoon on the radiator? Who is bending beside it to pray? You must learn that you can choose who you are branded by in this world. The small sounds of feet walking away from the bridge. The angel of mercy is rising from the tombs. Never forget dust to dust is what we are is stardust breathing. Dive deep into this world of shit and piss. The punctuation marks on your arms. Dear reader, I thank you for the most appropriate review for what I've learned through hard human decades is without the darkness how could we ever see the brightness of the one star we've become.

Sincerely,

Dear Editor, Who Solicited One Glenn Shaheen and Rejected Another,

Maybe they thought you were the other Glenn Shaheen, the one who lives in Louisiana or the one who is an engineer and writes short stories in his spare time, and stared at the white line on the page, or the one who died in Odessa, Texas, and afterwards his family drove out into the desert to scatter his remains in the place he used to sit, staring out at the horizon, waiting for his father to return from a war he never did. Perhaps they thought you were him and all the things he never said, and they didn't remember asking you or heard what they told themselves when they returned your pages. And in the end, how does so much of what we ask become ashes anyways?

Dear Reviewer Who Questions Confession,

I want to tell you my wife is off sipping surreptitiously on one of those little bottles they serve on airplanes she hides in our daughter's closet. She's looking good in her well-worn blue jeans. She lost her teeth from a disease. She used to have wounds on her feet. I'd like to say she started drinking then when she was in daily pain, but she probably started drinking with her first drink. My wife is un-fatigable trouble. She'd drink 24 hours a day if she could. She's the kind of woman they write honky-tonk country songs about. She's more Johnny Cash than the Dolly Parton she adores. She's the kind of woman blues musicians name their guitars after. Her favorite car is an El Camino. She's been trying to quit drinking after decades but even goes to her counseling sessions with a few good hard slugs in her. She counts hours not days between bottles. I wouldn't care honestly but she's going to die. Her pancreas is shot through with double fisted slugs like buckshot. She breathes whiskey. She's spritzed with Vodka. I swear she drinks perfume to cover the scent, but she denies this. She had an operation, a kind of miracle, that saved her last year. This old Jewish doctor from Pittsburgh ran a line through all her vital organs and drained a cyst off the back of her pancreas. It was enough to get me to believe in God. Now I pray to all the religion figures: Yahweh, Jesus, Shango, Krishna, burning incense for the Buddha when no one is around. The doctors told her if she kept drinking, she could die. But she doesn't listen. I carry that pain with me every day, that slow suicide right before my eyes with every twist of a cap, every shot glass slugged down in secret. Sometimes I fight with her, but you can't tell her anything. I threaten to leave her, ask her what our daughters would do. Our daughters are still children. My wife knows what is at stake but everything in this life is a dark joke to her. And then you are dead.

I remind her there is no joke after dead. I tell her I am writing her eulogy each day. Dear Reviewer, what can we know of anything passing as it passes? Lately she has stopped lying, trying to pretend she is sober as she slurs her words. She lets me take the car keys when she has had too much.

Everything has become hard. The late rain has turned to ice and snow. The great lake is beginning to freeze. I drive through my old neighborhood and stop and say a prayer beside the gold domed Russian church overlooking the giant freighter stationed for the winter in the bay. It is easier to handle dying in winter when everything is dead. There is a reason Eliot wrote spring is the cruelest month. Winter bandages the wounds we walk with in this world of grief. But it isn't grief I feel when I smell my wife's hair, it is something that we pass off as love but is so much more than can be said in any sentence, something that is part love and part desertion.

The Japanese have a word *utsuroi* that is not fully translatable but means something about the state of change, when an element passes from one state of matter into another, when beauty is passing. When a color shifts from pink to red? Once my wife wrote a poem about our daughter and the falling petals of a bonsai tree, this woman, getting drunk alone in the dark.

The light is always fleeting, or is it fleeing?

My wife is standing in the doorway between rooms.

She thinks I do not see her. Dear Reviewer, can you see her?

She is pink blossoms resting on a muddy puddle.

Let me tell you a story:

A woman raises
children
a woman raises
Cain/ to her lips a woman/ raises
whiskey/ raises
ruin/ raises
the rain/
back up into the clouds/

76

the rain travels
like pain through the chest
of a man who looks
out the window
away from the woman
to look away
and remain

like when rain
changes into wet snow
so heavy it bends
branches
almost to the ground
like an old woman
carrying buckets of water
strung on a pole
from the deepest well.

Dear HR Person from Health South Who Called,

to say I did not get the job, I did not mean offense when I laughed. How rare it is to hear back from a job application when we do not get the job. More often we hear nothing. In this century there is no long line waiting for work outside the plant to be told by a hard-faced foreman there are no shifts, no waiting for your script out on the dock. We walk with smoke in our skulls. We apply on line. We hit send. You write and send in your life on a page and hope for an interview and afterwards you hear nothing. So to get a call telling me that job went to someone else, I bet to that young woman with the long dark hair I met in the waiting room who looked like she could run a marathon, and well I suspected I was too old for the job when I saw the recruiter's eyes, though she did brighten when I said I knew how to make an excel file, and seemed impressed at my acknowledge of medications though she said I would we doing mostly PT, physical therapy and I thought of the lifting and my knees and maybe she saw me slightly wince, though by the end of the interview I still had hope but after two weeks I thought well that's that, and then you called. How many of us are out there waiting by the phone? We hear nothing. The only music I can write is written in the dust I do not sweep. There is a broom somewhere just my height, there is a box or person waiting for me to lift. No one even calls to say, no. No one points to us to say you are not needed, so I thank you for your call. Dear HR person, your voice tells me there is a file with my name, I nearly cry when you say, "It will be kept on file in case of any future openings we think that you will fit." Like a puzzle into a box, or a body into a ditch? We have become the invisible masses. We are out there waiting for the bus, as you pass on your morning commute. I want to say to you what Coleridge wrote, "Work without Hope draws nectar in a sieve,/ And Hope without an object cannot live." I am an object, with two hands and eyes. But I have vanished! In statistics, we are only seen if we ask the government for help. Once that check on Friday stops, no bureaucrat can say we are a number, a statistic that means we are waiting in rooms, sending out applications. This is not simply despair. What unearned wage we wear is weighed upon our shoulders? In the refrigerator is only milk and margarine, a pile of banquet meals. Any little we have we buy a bottle of something cheap. We stare out at the light that falls against a brick wall. The sirens howl all night. We turn back to the static in our brains. And what do we call ourselves these days? So many of the jobs we sell ourselves for contract wage? For temporary positions? Are we no longer workers? Waiting to be loaded in the back of a pick-up where nobody bothers to write down your name. For how long we say here are our bodies, take them. Make them bend. Give us our daily bread.

***Dear Book Contest Editor, Thank You for Your Letter Informing Me
My Manuscript Did Not Even Place.***

I never make the best of lists they have at the end of the year, even
after over a dozen books. Not one. But what did I expect from
literary life, it's not like I made a list before I was a writer? You know
those lists in high school for most popular, most likely best hair,
smile, most artistic, even the ones like one most likely to commit
a felony. But then I went to high school with several people who
were on lists like *Mr. Most Likely to Succeed:* Russ Muirhead who was a
Rhodes Scholar in Economics; *Most Athletic:* Chip Kelly who coached
the Philadelphia Eagles, and of course our *Class Comedian:* Adam
Sandler, renowned movie star and comedian who makes B list gems
and a bazillion dollars and I imagine is on every party list, you know
those Hollywood after hours after awards kind of clubs packed with
slip dressed models and expensive Vodka and pounds of cocaine on
the house. Yeah that list! Yee Haa! No wonder the word *list* comes
from the name for the area where knights would joust. But I've never
even made the list at the Polish Falcons social club to have my weekly
number drawn, never even been considered to win anything. Which
I suspect is the same for most everybody, except every now and then
someone's number is drawn, someone wins the lottery, someone
has the right six-digit number, someone has the right look, the right
name. And so, it goes. To be on the list is to be on the rung to the
spectacular, to cover our bodies with glitter and stars. To walk the
runway. To be known and exclaimed. A list. To be a hit on the hit list.
The hit list, of course in a different context is the last place you want
to be. Or the wanted list, your face postered on every post office wall.
Hiding out in seedy motels, a 9-millimeter tucked in a waist band,
and a dubious cause tattooed across your chest. To enlist is to go to
war. We go to war every day. We make our lists we bucket them down,
all the things we'll never do because we work sixty hours a week and
our kids need things, and our spouses are drunk. We go to bars and
drink too much and list to the right off the road. Dear wife,

when you were sickest, and I thought you weren't coming home I
found the last grocery list we made: palaak paneer, eggs, a slinky,
milk, cat food, egg molds, broccoli—it made no sense. But we have
not made sense since we first listed into one another's arms, strung
out and lost. There is no list for how I hope or what I carry through

this life, no list I could make to explain after all these years my ribs still play like a broken xylophone our discordant song,

I am still brainstorming what to do, what chores to check off and complete? What urgent reply to send to what Dear Editor, can I tell you of our work except we live along the lake far from anywhere where we would be on a list, never to be invited to the latest best seller release, never to drink martinis with New York editors in that penthouse far from hospital ER rooms, far from rehabs, far from morgues where our murdered friends were taken, far from heroin and OD's far from our old found dead alone in rented rooms. What list can we make for them Dear Editor? What list for us the invisible, the workers with our nightshifts and our shovels? With our bullet strewn:

• foreclosed houses

• unpaid mortgage (mort the root of death)

• What is there for us,

• the average, the unspectacular

• working for minimum wage,

• the unbonded, the uninsured, the undocumented

• not on any list,

• the taken and the disappeared,

• the voices no one hears

• when He reads off our names

• they will sing loud

• from the pages of the book

• bent backed lepers each of us

• will enter the Kingdom of God

• and we will tell him there was no Eden.

Dear Editor, Who Wrote, "Thank You for the Chance to Read Your Work. Unfortunately, We Can't Use It at This Time,"

I used to help take care of this guy named Danny who was obsessed with time. He liked to collect clocks. He had a row of clocks on the bureau by his bed. He liked to set the alarms and have them all go off and drive staff crazy. It was amazing how he did it because the clocks were set for a dozen different times and somehow, he synchronized the alarms. Danny had Down Syndrome and lived at the residential house I worked at on an on-call basis. Danny was barely five feet tall. He had lived on his own for decades, worked as a bagger at the Giant Eagle grocery until they phased out bag boys. Did you ever wonder what happened to those people after they went to mostly self-serve checkout? What was Danny to do? He loved shoes. He had a closet full of shoes. Danny was small, and it turns out he had figured out he could crawl through the ventilation system of his apartment, like a ninja. He would crawl into the apartments next door and take shoes, maybe one at a time, take shiny things like a jewel thief, or a myna bird. But after he was laid off, he grew sad and fat and one day he got stuck in the vent between his apartment and the next. The neighbors heard him yelling through the wall. When the paramedics arrived and dislodged him, it solved the great mystery in the complex, that had plagued its residents, of the magical disappearance of missing things. When the police arrived, they found in his apartment hundreds and hundreds of shoes, fat laced adidas, red high heels, children's slippers, old lady bunny ears, and a box full of jewelry, the real stuff and the costume all mixed up. It was the shine he had taken too. He didn't care about the cost. I can't remember if he was charged or not. Danny was far from dumb. He surmised long ago what he could get away with. He calculated the figures, he managed the odds. He liked wrestling paraphernalia and had the costume of Hulk Hogan and an actual belt that some wrestler had given him when he went to the Sports Arena for a minor league wrestling extravaganza. Danny had learned early on that having Down Syndrome could get you stuff. He was the consummate hustler. He was always trying to get $5 off me. Loan me $5 so I can get some food. These people here are STARVING ME. When I first met him, he asked me, do you know who Sharon Stone is, she's a friend of mine. I said, yes, she's a movie star, she was terrific in Casino acting alongside Deniro. Deniro the bum, Danny said. She carried him the whole way. He said, she calls me all the time. I looked at his regular staff who just smiled as if to say, here we go again. He said, ok she calls me every Christmas. I looked at other staff who were no longer listening and didn't look up from their cell phones. Danny took my hand and walked me to the bookshelf in the common area and pulled down a giant picture book. It was a book of celebrities with portraits of people with Down Syndrome who had impacted their lives or were friends or family's members of them. He flipped the pages and there he was with Sharon Stone. Turns out Sharon Stone had been his baby sitter when he was a kid. She had written in the text, Danny taught me so much about being confident, he was even then a trickster full of kindness. Danny beamed. Danny was starting to get dementia. He was starting to forget. People with Down Syndrome can get dementia early. He was only 49. I had to remind him what day it was, the small details were leaving him. One day I arrived at work and he appeared in the common area in full wrestling regalia, like Hulk Hogan shrunk to size, leather tasseled jacket and championship gold belt around his waist. How do I look he asked? I said, you look like a superhero.

After decades of having a job, of having a license, I found out the final reason Danny could not live by himself was not his trickster ways but was because of his dementia. It is always the little forgetfulnesses that do us in. One day before leaving to go shopping he had started to run a bath then forgot to get in and left his apartment. He didn't turn the water off. The water reached the top of the tub and overflowed and kept on going like something from a State Farm Insurance commercial, before it flooded the apartment and ran out into the hall. The fire department came and broke the door down and shut the water off, but the apartment was ruined. After that his case manager said he needed to live in a home, he needed someone to care for him. In Danny's room at the residential house was a row of clocks, each set for a different time. When I looked at them, I wondered what elegies arrive for us with every passing minute?

Danny, your clocks are all set at random different times, doesn't that drive you crazy. He looked at me and said, no they are set for every time zone at sunrise and sunset around the world. Well I'll be. Whether this was true or not I did not know. He was a trickster. He liked to make up things. I never got the chance to check if it was true. I think at the time I was only half listening, trying to surreptitiously find another resident's size 10 sneaker that had come up missing in Danny's giant pile of shoes.

Sincerely,

Dear Editor, Who Sent Me a Rejection Letter on Christmas (or Essay That Ends in a Fugue),

At first, I was like for real, man. Really? But then I immediately thought of my coworker Wayne, whose wife died a few years ago near Christmas, and what dismal days the holidays are for him, each colored light blinking on every house a stop light for this life, a demarcation, a calling back to a kind of grief that with each passing year keeps going on. This week he was a bitter mess, slamming the phone down repeatedly when it wouldn't let him punch in, the automated system overloaded for some minutes, cursing to himself over the smallest detail of the day—a missed signature, a food item used a day too early. I caught him staring off many times, remembering, or recalling perhaps her face, a smell, perhaps an exchange of tender words. Such a strange hell memory can be, and the irony is that the people we take care of cannot sometimes remember their age or where they live. There is something to be said for not remembering. I used to think of memory as something to define us, to tell us who we are, but often it too can be something to keep us from living in the present tense. We live back there in a place that does not exist. Eurydice in the far distance fading back

to the underworld. The world that disappears with each passing instant. She lived and now she doesn't. It really is that simple. I thought this so many years of my own wife, the long nights in the hospital, wondering if this hour would be the last, the slow morphine drip of time passing when one is in pain. Memory is like this:

but Wayne gets the details right when he needs to, remembers one of our patients doesn't like ham, buys him turkey for Christmas dinner out of his own pocket and brings him a plate, one of our long term difficult patients who I know Wayne doesn't even like, but "like" has little to do with us in this job—to care for those for no other reason than care is what is called for.

And this Dear Editor, reminds me that grief can bring one towards the untold deep-ness of compassion, like the failing promise of this Christmas day. Jesus born only to be crucified on the cross. In the end we are all failures, we are all grieving someone, or something gone.

And perhaps Dear Editor you need to walk away from the screen.
Stop sending out rejections. Go outside, and look up into the sky

at all that quiet tenderness bandaging the earth. Each day we go on
we leave something far
behind us

flapping like laundry on a cord strung line
in the backyard of a stranger.

Perhaps this is not about those we love
but about those we do not know
but show compassion
which is perhaps what love is
anyways at its finest: hollow and calm
as the inside of a bell,
we get to work, we feel only the echo
of the other—

And when they are gone? What do we have left?

Not the place of saints, who exist outside themselves. No, compassion
and love are the traits of ordinary women and men.

Soon enough the new year will arrive. Wayne will rise each morning,
brush his teeth, shower, dress, arrive to pass out medications. He will
flip through the pages of the photos of his wife when he is alone in
the office, the hand collaged journal I found in a desk drawer when
I was looking for a bottle of Advil we keep for staff. What does all of
this mean you ask?

Wayne wears his grief like the hair shirts
of saints, but what he wants to reassemble
are the shattered pieces of a life
he cannot glue back together,
though he tries each day to reframe the window

he finds himself sieved
with mourning light
like stained glass figures
missing hands.

Those hands that touched our foreheads and made us soup.

Between compassion and failure there is a bridge.
Grief is a river that runs between our worlds.
Between forgetting and remembrance there is a bridge
that leads to a house by the embankment.
Ghosts crossing many rooms
like stained glass figures missing hands.
Wayne dives into his grief like a river
running between two worlds
there is a glass bell
sieved with mourning light.
It has been four years
since his wife died on a hospital bed
the toll it has taken on him
is a life he cannot abandon
is a bridge between failure
and the compassion of ordinary
women and men. What do we have to mend?
Soon enough the new year will arrive
flapping like laundry on a cord strung line
in the backyard of a tenement
fenced with colored Christmas lights.
A blow-up Santa strung up like Jesus.

Dear Editor, Who Sent Me a Rejection Letter on New Year's Day,

I want to be mean and name you the killer of hope, but since I worked 60 hours this week at my facility passing medications and dealing with outbursts like waking the new man John up in the morning and I say to him, John it's morning time to get up and get showered and he says I don't give a fuck, and I say you really should get up, I'll get you some coffee and he says I don't give a fuck and I say John I know it's not light out, it's this damn thing called winter, it's the earth man, it's the sun and earth conspiring to keep you in bed and even the birds are probably dead this morning, John the birds have all flown away, there is no singing. John today is the death of music! And then I switch on his stereo and Def Leopard of all things fills his room, and he says O for fucking fuck's sake, and I know I have him and he swings half a leg off the bed. This is how it is, and I received your letter right about the time I would be there, getting these men up with their brain injuries, but instead I am home reading your rejection letter, my first of the New Year, a year which was supposed to begin with hope. A year after a year where my girlfriend finally almost died down in a hospital in Pittsburgh but instead was saved by this ancient little Jewish doctor who pulled off a Torah kind of miracle and we got married and then she tried to drink herself to death but decided not to, despite my pleading to put me out of my misery and all things they come to pass, the pissing and the pain, it goes Dear Editor. It returns. And this your letter has reminded me of that, reminded me of how cruel hope is, and not to cling to it. I read a story this week about a stranger who gave a child a piece of their liver to save his life, this woman did not know this child and gave that organ for nothing but good will but then even though all things said it should have been a match, it was rejected. And the child died. What can save the body is seen as a foreign object, like a stone or a knife. Because this is how it goes in this life all the numbers can say this is good, but the day turns into a wake. This is one reason I have been asleep for decades. After I got your letter Dear Editor, I thought this man is working too hard teaching and finally today on his day off on his break he is trying to catch up, he is shaking off his hangover, he is clearing his que. Last night since I've been working so much overtime I stood in a long que at the supermarket and waited as we slowly moved, a dozen strangers with their carts of shrimp circles and lobster, their party hats, their crème brûlée, and brought home my family some expensive steaks to celebrate we made it to another year. We ate those steaks with potatoes and onions and peppers. My oldest daughter who is autistic ate that meat with her fingers. I said to my wife, it is good she likes it a little rare. In this world it is better to taste the blood and bite down harder to prepare you for its pain.

Sincerely,

Dear Those Who Died by Rejection,

No not injection. The child whose body rejected the liver, whose body claimed death rather than to accept what could be healed. Or the heart cut out of the body after the car accident. The 32-year-old man in California who checked the right box and they cut his heart out and packed it in ice and shipped it by courier in a jet across the continent where a team of emergency surgeons was called to stitch it into the body of a teenage girl, a girl with lots of life ahead of her who was born with a faulty aorta. And afterwards there was weeping and healing, and six months later she was walking, she was taking her pills her anti-rejection and seizure meds. And then one morning she wakes up dead, clutching her chest, her body rejecting what it was given. A sense of dread there at the edge of the playground is the teenage girl. They call her names since she was in second grade. They say words like slut or dyke, and you should be dead. They say this for no reason other than they can. She hung herself from a cord. Her mother found her hanging there. Her name was Tamara. She liked to draw. She drew herself in blacks and blues and always there were yellow stars were her eyes should be. Gold stars placed on paper charts in schools, gold stars sewn on chests. Scarlet letters, head wraps, stones that fall from unrepentant hands. Some God said you did not follow the rules. I read once the neuro-scientists believe rejection activates in our brains the same synapses as physical pain, as if we were bruised. The social scientists think it is evolutionary, how hard rejection hurts us, it forced us to cling to the tribe, to survive. But what happens when we are shunned. My Jewish grandfather was shunned by his family because he married a woman who was not Jewish. Even on his death bed his brother would not speak to him. They sat Shiva in their hearts for seven decades. What makes one see a human being as less than, what is rejection but a form of violence and fear? All the clean shaven and shunned Amish in towns across Pennsylvania, posting posters for day labor at every dive. How are they to survive? Reach your hand out to the other. They have five fingers same as you, or is it three? Two blown off by a land mine? Hold the absence of two fingers. Press that absence to your lips. They cover their heads. Their heads are not covered. They love someone who looks like them. They love someone who does not look like them. They love a book, a man, a woman, a different God.

91

A faceless God. A God with a face. The socials scientists screwed up. It is not rejection that calls us to the tribe. It is what the tribe uses to claim its privileged space. Rejection is a weapon, is a fact, not a theory. You cannot work for us. You will not get that wage. The phone does not ring. The boy does not call after you gave him your body. He is laughing at the ball field with his friends. He names you a bad name. The name follows you down the long hall like a ghost in an abandoned strip mall. They write the name on bathroom stalls. It cannot be erased. But the only thing that can't be erased is what is truly human. The body pushes back, the body arches its back to strike. Unloose the noose, put down the bottle of pills. Unload the chamber to the gun. Pull up the suicide shade. Who wants to be a sphere attached to other spheres, circling in endless ellipticals? Who wants to be part of a system? Rejection can mean freedom, not prison. Unlock the gate, we are leaving this town. I always envied the comet, its untamed light, how it blazes its brilliant trail of ice and rock across the cosmos pulled by and toward a greater gravity.

Dear Editor, Who Admitted He Fears His Inbox,

I used to fear my composition papers. As a matter of fact, that may be the top reason I stopped teaching, that end of the semester anxiety buried under piles I grew less and less able to approach. It became something about time, a fear of time known as *chronophobia.* I became aware of every second of this life passing through me, like a soft wind rippling over water that was rising. And the piles grew larger, became something more than piles but something about me as a man, my ability or inability to maintain a decent wage, to make a comment, to offer suggestions that meant something that helped. There must be a word for this. There is a word for every kind of fear. There is *papyrophobia,* the fear of paper. It sounds silly, this fear. But then I found out how common it is. Thousands perhaps even millions of people suffer from this. My daughter who has Asperger's is terrified of the feel of paper. She must wear gloves to complete her homework. The sound of pencils to her too is like scratching nails across a chalkboard. The name for this fear of selected sounds is called *misophonic.* We all have this to some degree I suspect, the sound of a person's voice even. Dear Editor, I cannot tell you how many male teaching colleagues I had who when they spoke their endless self-aggrandizing monologues, I wanted to poke out my own eyes. Perhaps there is a tone to everything in this world, an aura and a hymn, a tone and a tempo. Sometimes it is what makes us hum. Sometimes it makes us want to crawl out of our skin. But then there is paper. There is even a fear called *formaphobia* which is the fear of "official" paperwork: doctors and tax forms, welfare papers! And why not? For bureaucracy is a form of death machine, the right or wrong paper sent or not sent or done wrong or sent too late and your children starve. Lord knows how many times we argued with social services or the taxman. What is there not to fear? Which is the larger question because it would be so easy to fear everything and not climb out of this bed, but I suspect the way we judge our courage in this life is to overcome the smallest things. My wife says she has a fear of laundry, or maybe she said it is of wrinkled clothes. She hides her Vodka in the overflowing baskets and drinks it straight when the kids are loud. The kids are loud a lot. Which brings me back to piles, all those clothes piled in laundry baskets. And all of these gets at things we did not have to worry about when humans were worried about what to hunt, to fish, to eat. We did not have granaries to fill or papers to check, or quotas to meet. We did what we did, and we did it. But then I realize that is naïve Neolithic aggrandizement because of course the image comes of women washing clothes with stones in a creek. This labor that always ate our days. The fears of being able simply to maintain. And those fears grow until we cannot even read what it is our job to write, or bake or make, or even touch another human being.

I take care of a man who suffers from *haphephobia,* the fear of touch. He is a big white man in his late forties, over six feet tall with ink black hair. He is never quiet, talking a rambling mish-mash of memories and cooking suggestions. He spent all his time in the kitchen before his brain injury. He loved to cook. He loved to make *Cincinattitttiiiii Chilllllieee.* He draws it out like that every time he says it. He loves to say the word cinna*mon.* He says the last syllable round as if he is saying mom. He speaks with his hands and takes up a grand amount of space but if you even brush his hand or forget and touch his shoulder lightly, he will freak out and jump like the Tasmanian devil, stamping his foot and twirling as he makes a series of shrieks and high-pitched squeaks. It is like you are an electrical socket and his body is a conductor of shocks. The other men feared him for a long time, but everyone here finds their range. Plus, his nonsense is musical and funny. *I love to scramble eggs,* he says. *I love to whisk them in a frying pan like whiskey with a little cinnamon and salt and gulp them down.* He suffers from a fear of germs too, known as *mysophobia* and is obsessive compulsive. He carries a small vile of hand cleanser with him everywhere. But the fear of touch the nurses tell us is something else. It isn't just people but certain feels. He cannot stand the vinyl couch. He sneakers must be leather. When his family visits they never hug him. His sister says that not wanting to be touched began after his injury. He goes through life alone now alongside others. Imagine never being held? Imagine never wanting to be held? To part the air possessive of no one by one's self. Perhaps there is a certain freedom to this, or is it simply fear? Luckily, he does not suffer from a fear of being alone, known as *autophobia* which does not even just mean

94

physically alone, but the fear of being unloved. If anything, like most of the injured, his ability for empathy to others has been damaged. This is what we work on them the most. The verbal thankyous, and blessyous. Not to punch the wall when you aren't first for meds. The world is not your skin. Other bodies have feelings. If they cannot learn this, they cannot leave the grounds and go back to their lives. If he trusts you, he will tell you he has special powers. He says we all have these powers, but he has learned to harness them. He says, *everything is electric*. He said he is learning how to become invisible, that one day I will arrive, and he will have vanished. Where will you go, I ask? He always points toward outside and says, *of course, where else but elsewhere?* Is there a word for the fear of disappearing? One moment we are here and now we are gone. Not a fear of death, but something else. In Japan it is estimated over 100,000 people have "disappeared" themselves due to mounting debt. They sell what they have left and vanish to live a life someplace else in penance or flagellation. One man I read lives in a windowless room and drinks his daily dose of despair. I read in the New York Post "Another case, unresolved, involved the young mother of a disabled 8-year-old boy. On the day of her son's school musical, in which he was performing, the mother disappeared — despite promising the boy she'd be sitting in the front row. Her seat remained empty. She was never seen again. Her husband and child agonize; the woman had never given any indication she was unhappy, in pain, or had done something she thought wrong." I believe that words have a shape and if we say them right, they can recall what is gone. I listen for the messenger. Sometimes I think the men I care for hear it. Out there in the wind and rain. In the morning mist, before the nurses arrive, it hovers just above the dew-drenched grass. This I must admit Dear Editor is my deepest fear, one that I could not bear to name: losing my wife or our daughters, not by abandonment but to be disappeared, without cause or closure, and then one appears on those posters for the missing that tattoo the post office walls. No wonder so many of us are terrified of paper.

Dear Piles of No from All the Usual Suspects,

And of course, at first, I mean this picture my friend posted on Facebook of piles of rejection letters she had saved in envelopes from back in the days when we mailed out our work and the nos came back on little slips of paper. We tape-collaged them on the walls above our desks or even one friend who really did plaster his bathroom, or another friend who would push them into little piles of no from all the usual suspects, on his concrete back porch and then drink too much whiskey and turn them into little SS-like bonfires. He'd write a poem in the ashes with his finger that would sit there on his porch for the postman delivering rejection letters to read, until the rain came and washed it away. Perhaps all the true poems should be written to last only until the rains arrive. The rain of No. All the usual suspects, such as our fifth grade teacher who took the poem the girl wrote a poem in the dark shape of her father's hand and said Don't be too dramatic, and I asked you to write a poem in the shape of a Christmas tree, or our religious parent who burned our notebook, our friends who laughed, our bosses, our foreman. I think how once I took a taxi ride across the Bronx, passed bodegas and pawnshops, around and under the El, trying to find this tiny Dominican joint to meet my friend Tony, and the Afghani cab driver named Nouman for no exact reason I can recall (maybe I said we were going to a poetry reading) asked me, do you know the poet Hafiz and recited to me first in Urdu and then in English, "Do you know how beautiful you are/ when you sit in the shadow of the friend." We were caught in crosstown traffic and the address I had was wrong, we drove up the side of buildings and up fire escapes, to the rooftops where old men raised pigeons and marijuana groves, drove through mercados and stole avocados and drove away, drove over the water and back to his home in Lashkar, passed the burnt out Mosque and the place he buried his youngest daughter, over the landmine that took his left hand, and his brother. Passed the wreckage burning on the horizon, the plumes of black ash. He told me how the men without uniforms arrived in pickup trucks came to his village and the piles of bodies, and that it was poetry that taught him all life goes away, all life returns. Here he handed me a picture of his youngest daughter with her hands raised above her head. She was dancing. Take me to the ocean I said. I want to smell the ocean. We drove across the Grand Concourse, out to Pelham Bay. He parked the cab. He said, after they murdered the village elders, I learned no one ever really dies. There where our dead were piled and buried in ditches, months later when the rains finally arrived, poppies bloomed on the hillsides. They were like lanterns lighting the inside of the earth.

Sincerely,

Dear Rejection Killer,

Not one who makes rejection go away. Not one who strangles the anger. Invent a boyfriend, memorize fake numbers to give, fake email, fake Facebook page. Is this the sort of thing you think of in the United States? The doctor who was stabbed by her fiancé. The woman in Detroit shot when she said her boyfriend was inside the wedding the reception. The kind of murders of sexual retribution that take place in some far-off tribal Pakistani retaliation for not wanting to marry, or adultery. But in the United States last year hundreds were murdered simply for *rejecting male advances*. The records are under reported. Years ago, in a nightclub I saw a man punch a woman in the jaw simply for saying, I'm not dancing with you. She fell to the floor. To mistake envy. Soon sirens. The bouncer dragged him out. I heard other men hiss, *bitch* as the stretcher arrived. The right to resist your own death. In the eyes of others to not be able to do what you want. In the eyes of others to become object, or prey. It is so common it has a name, *Rejection Killings*. Even the stillness is skeletal. Biblical in its tone I think of women being stoned for adultery. Could it begin with a catcall? Stanzas going deaf. A whistle? The 29-year-old man who showed up at the teenager's house and shot her? Shemel Mercurius loved blue. She wanted to be a veterinarian. She loved to walk through Brooklyn streets. She sang as she walked her sister said. She was shot three times by a man she'd only meet in passing a week before. There is a bloody light that falls through the trees in summer. She was shot for saying no. Many of these men were casual acquaintances. That man who places a hand on you on the subway, the bus. Do you even say thank you for holding the door? Now he is walking beside you. Anything I can do to save us splits. To let means to take or cut. You glance around, does anyone care? You look for a bathroom. You sit on the toilet inside the stall so long you miss your bus. To pass by a group of men working on the street, hanging at the basketball court, in the courtyard. Look, don't look. Do not become the dead woman in the crumpled news. Say something, say nothing. Walk faster. Should I run? Lauren McKwen writes "Two years ago a teenage boy threw a bottle of water at me, because I, an adult, would not give him my phone number. It struck me square in the back. This happened in broad daylight on a busy Washington, D.C. street, with plenty of onlookers. No one said a word. My back ached for days."

The man was so shriveled he became enraged. The little skull inside his brain. What is the wound that cannot heal? 17-year-old Dimitrios Pagourtzis shot 10 students and teachers at Santé Fe high because Ana Fisher turned him down, embarrassed him when he wouldn't leave her alone. The car that pulls up beside you, catcalling. The bloody map on the butcher's apron. After she slept with you. After the phone did not ring. After her perfume, her scent, caught you, you dug down to that dark place to find your reason, to justify your weapon. You named her nothing like her name. There were three finches sitting on the fence where they found her. None of them were singing. No one said she knew him. She had passed by a door, she was waiting in the same line at the Doller General, she sat in the same college class, she turned the wrong way at the wrong time on the wrong day. He is there waiting. There is no reason to define these circumstances. There is nothing to address. Dear rejection killer, what if only she had or had not said whatever it was or never was she said?

CODA:

see them

the ghost women,

thin as gauze they

rise above the lake,

a burial shroud

of fog drifts

like a breath

from lips, saying

no.

Dear Lymphocytes,

Who decides what the body can accept? The pain that causes breath? The slammed door, the phone call that decides your bread? We sleep with one eye open to our dead, a murmurous train of dread. For what we are speaking about is remaining in this light and space, or leaving for another world? To think there is something we cannot see who may decide this all? But that is the oldest claim? The hand, the spirit, the guides? The invisible lines we travel on towards or through desire? The flame inside the fire? The name inside the flame? On the tiniest level there are these cells that decide whether an organ transplant will take, or what will activate the antigens. The piss turns dark, the body aches then seizes. The body will not claim the organ but that as other. We do this in this life, we call a friend sister, name them brother. But who is stranger than those close to us, who causes us the damage most? The body will not accept the host.

My friend Ken had a liver transplant the body would not take. The years of drinking caught him after fifty. Ken was a big man, over six foot four. He worked building diesel engines. One night at the social club he came out of the restroom spread his arms and said, I'm pissing blood. He bought another round. These cells called Lymphocytes in his thyroid begin the process of attacking the introduced tissue. It names them other. It is part of how we have evolved, the body's way of defending itself. He had three kids, two boys and a girl named Sara who died of an overdose at seventeen. One son, Jimmy, works with him at the plant. Ken said, the hardest was to go on for the others after she died. You want to drown yourself, you want. He bought another round. It is rejection on the cellular level? It is perhaps the reason we have fences. We cannot read the faces of the other. We cannot find the right match. Ken's transplant was a near match but not near enough. His lymphocytes in his thyroid activated the antigens and began to damage his liver. The organ given by a stranger, who had marked a box who thought to save a life upon his or her own death, that light that shines, without grieving or regret, they cut the body open, packed and ice and brought it a bright home where it was stitched and sewn in place. Six months later Ken's piss grew dark, his belly swelled, his skin yellowed. It was winter. The last time I saw him he was sitting up in a hospital bed, he told me he was thirsty. I poured him a glass of water. He told me a story. He said when he was a kid, maybe ten years old, he and his friends found a bee's nest by the fence where they played baseball. The ball had rolled right next to the nest, just a hole in the sand. They were these tiny little bees he said, we called them sand bees. I don't know if they have another name. No one wanted to get the ball, but I went to get it, I thought those little bees can't hurt me. I reached my hand and picked the ball up and then for some reason I kicked the sand into their hive. And then they swarmed. I ran slapping at the air. My face and arms were covered with stings. I barely made it out of there. Funny how some things so small can hurt so bad. I don't know why I kicked that sand? He stared out the window at the frozen bay. The doctors came in with their chart and I walked away. I pressed the button and watched the elevator doors close. I never saw Ken alive again. We all are in some way lymphocytes in this world, we push and pull against those foreign agents we deem who would be our demise. The scientists would never say this but there is fierceness and fear in these cells. We are programmed with a purpose and design. Our body is our body, our breath our breath. Dear lymphocytes, is there a form of you as air and light? Can thought and spirit be a form of cell? Can this explain why sometimes we murder what would save us.

We the Editors,

First, we erased the Dodo, the Tasmanian Tiger, the black rhino, the Ibex. Then even the common beasts were red inked: the carrier pigeon, the bison, the eastern wolf, the white nosed deer, the European badger. An endless bulleted list. We checked them off and put a sad face on the article. It showed we cared. We edited out everything. Then we edited the genes of what was left. Imagined rewriting them back for no reason other than we could. Our own sequel to our prequel. The wooly Mammoth, the great whales, Neanderthal man. Imagine the domed Paleolithic theme park, the tickets we could sell? We bottled the water, sold it back to ourselves. Sipped it politely at the doctor's office as we edited our children. We red inked the ones who could not speak, or hear, or see, or walk, the different, the ugly, were never born. Everything became legend, animated. Nothing existed except behind a screen. Kindness disappeared, compassion evaporated like the lakes. We marched onward. Empathy became processed and plastic. Another tool to auction off the objects we must own. We spoke only in characters of grotesque human faces. Words vanished. All that was left were the yellow song birds, stoic high above the carnage, they sat like notes to a dirge on the highest wires crisscrossed above our heads, until that day we looked up from our shining screens *thud thud, thud thud,* to witness the rain of small feathered bodies plummeting—

And something strange and unexpected happened, we put down our devices and reached out to catch them in our hands, and a few of them with tiny hearts barely beating, we fed them tap water with a spoon. We held them to our chests, we kept our eyes on them, till one by one a few not dead began to speak a tune, a cluster of furious notes, and then tentative at first they flew, but now they would not leave us, and for the first time in decades we saw the sky, high above, and we hopped on our motor-trikes to the wasteland to witness the stars and with our fingers we drew against the dark, but this time it was the dark we felt, how it had been inside us all along. The space between things. We dug our hands into the dirt. We rubbed it on our chests. And the oldest ones of us brought out the contraband of seeds. And after the rains came, we saw the first seedlings sprout and the death light of the far away cities. We were a tribe of many faces.

We carried parakeets upon our shoulders. We found the hidden boxes and unfolded the ancient recipes for making soup and bread. We learned again the songs from long ago. And soon more arrived. We blessed the earth. We made our own flags from tattered sheets. And we waited for them to come, for even if we failed, we knew the end was near for them who had been us. The birds blessed us, and we feed them holy water. We harvested the seeds. We wore molted feathers in our hair. We took again our tribal names. We learned again to make our drums. We painted our faces with lines and swirls. The future and the past joined in one circle we danced together joining hands. With our stomps, we raised the dust. The dust that we are made of. We would learn again how to bury our dead.

Dear Editor, Who Returned My Essay Covered with Sticky Notes,

Like the ones we use at work to remind ourselves of things mundane and important, such as L tried to steal sugar from the kitchen, or J is out of toilet paper and wiping herself with her hand, or P's blood pressure is high and to notify nursing. At the end of each shift you can see the staff's trail for the day in yellow squares of hastily scrawled blue or black ink (the state mandates all documents must be done in black or blue). We then translate our notes into documentation on official tracking papers called IDAPS (Individual daily activity plan). This lets the caseworker and the state know how our people are doing. We then collect those sticky notes into a log entry to tell the oncoming staff what is happening in the house. It all sounds chaotic and it is, but it is how we communicate, how we keep track of the lives of the men and women we watch over, when we are short of time and nearly always understaffed. It is how we remind ourselves, these notes, of what happened in the blur of requests and call offs, of giving medications, of outbursts and tantrums, all the short circuiting of the brain injured, all the CTOs, which means Consideration to others, the small things they might do that show empathy, handing each other a cup or holding a door or saying please and thank you, these are hard for them, the frontal lobe damage makes the lives of others hard to see, but we see. We write them down on yellow sticky notes, we mark the smallest gestures. It tells us they are getting better, or they are remembering at least what it is to be a person who can see someone other than themselves.

~

My wife likes to use sticky notes on the fridge. So does her mother. I tell my wife I can tell when she is drunk by how legible her notes are. She writes Milk, Pop, Lettuce, and I know she is sober. She writes something that looks like Hambergah, Funch Feirs, I know she has either become Danish or Dutch or she has been hitting on a fifth of Vodka she hides around the house. I love her sticky notes. I love the ones she writes on our children. Once I found one that simply said Mittens. It was so simple and tender I nearly wept. It was late October and she was thinking ahead. It might have read in the space around the letters, I love my children and I promise I will not die.

When she was most sick, when she had wounds on her feet and was in the hospital for weeks, I would find her grocery lists. I could not bear to throw them away. I have a drawer full of the lists of the most mundane things: frosted flakes, ketchup, pork chops, bread crumbs, pierogi. Perhaps this is all love really is—the simple daily inscriptions we give and let go: shopping, washing clothes, a passing brush of a hand, mowing the lawn. Everything we hate to do is part of this. We do the chores, we go to work. We lend a hand. This is what our brain says. Luther Vandross sings "A chair is still a chair, even when there's no one sittin' there/ But a chair is not a house and a house is not a home." What is a home? After the arguments and the pleading, after the nights alone and the cops knocking on the door. Between the children screaming and the laughter, between the long hours of work and fighting with the government about disability checks, after the bills have been sorted, at the end of it all, dolls and Legos left out on the carpet, dishes that still need to be done, taking out the trash to the curb in the cold. I walk back into the house; our daughters are in bed. My wife draws a heart on a sticky note and places it on my head.

Sincerely,

Dear UPMC Hamot, Birthing Department,

BOY was I happy when I received your email saying you'd like to interview me for the job in the Neonatal Department, helping with births and taking ADLS and helping the nurses to manage the floor. I applied for the job because I pictured each day of newborn babies, tying balloons, shaking the hands of relatives, checking the blood pressure and oxygen levels of new mothers' breast feeding for the first time, as they gleamed with the miraculous thread of light that connects their bodies to the bodies of the born. I thought of all the cool scrubs I'd wear, ones with Looney Tunes, Elmer Fudd, Scooby Doo, what's her name from Frozen that my daughter dressed up for like a year. I'd wear yellow smiley-face scrub hats like when my youngest daughter was born, the doctor who leaned over my girlfriend's body and said here she is. The shining light of it all.

But then I remembered the blood that day, and something went wrong, and how my girlfriend turned pale, the blood that covered the floor, and the techs not being able to stop the pain and I kept calling her name, but she could not answer, and I thought she was dead. And the day my oldest daughter was born three months too early, so small I could hold her in the palm of my hand, and the months we visited her in the NQ unit, the tubes that riddled her body, and how I prayed, I mean really prayed, as around us other mothers were weeping for their children who could not be saved.

Like the day your email arrived Dear Recruiter, I told my colleague Sheryl, a one on one Caregiver and CNA, who told me, "I used to work on the birthing floor at the Cleveland Institute, I helped out at the desk. I'll never forget that Christmas at 1:45 AM when the first child was born. And then she wasn't breathing. She was breach birthed and it was bad, and the doctors could not get her to breathe. I've never heard someone cry that long and hard, all through the night. The nurses let the mother hold her daughter for a while, hold her on her chest, and then she had to let her go. What do you do with a memory like that? I didn't work there long afterwards. Some things are just too much, that sort of grief, even if it isn't your own. Just to know it."

What could I say? I popped all the invisible balloons I was holding in my hand. I thought of my first wife's miscarriages, of my girlfriend's lost child, of my friend the professor whose son was still born, and the grief was so deep she gave up teaching and moved her life far away to work on a farm, to tend to goats, and grow blueberries and corn, to be close as can be to the living and dying things of this earth.

CODA

Dear Recruiter, I have reconsidered my application and cannot accept your kind invitation to interview. Today it is sunny along the lake, after a night of heavy snow, and I am helping my daughters to put on their coats and mittens. They told me they want to build a snowchild, no taller than their small heads. It will stand outside alone in the cold. We will pack its body with our hands. And afterwards as my daughters sit inside and sip their coco, I will think of their lost sister, the snowy lawn criss crossed with their boot prints like absent children.

Dear Editor, Who Sent Me a Tiered Rejection,

Which made me wonder if it was the 3rd tier or the 1st, and how good it felt not to be in the 133rd row for a change, but really when I got your note it felt more like I was under the bleachers at the night school basketball game when I was 14, where I was greeted with my first kiss by Katie Dowd, before she walked away and sat with her friends, and drank a bottle of Robitussin, and ended up kissing my best friend before puking under the bleachers in the same spot where we had stood and her buddy Donna and I carried her arm and arm out into the winter night and on towards home. I never kissed her again but even then I knew like this rejection Dear Editor, not all rejections are the same, and some, well they are a kind of hope, the way the stars are a kind of hope, so far in the dark there above the railroad tracks and the tenements and a gymnasium, emptying out with the last stragglers and quips and hollers of those years so long ago before we'd ever even fallen—

Credits and Acknowledgements

Some of these pieces were published or are forthcoming in the following journals, sometimes under different titles or versions.

About Place Journal: "Dear Editor, Who Wrote Thank You for the Chance to Read Your Work,"; "Dear Editor, Who Returned My Poems and Said They Weren't Taking Submissions but Didn't Tell Me When to Submit,"

Birmingham Poetry Review: "Dear Piles of No from All the Usual Suspects,"

Bitter Oleander: "We the Editors,"

Blue Earth Review: "Dear Editor, Who Said My Work Was Too Narrative for Their Journal,"; "Dear Reviewer, Who Questions Confession,"

Brevity: "Dear Editor, Who Made the Remarks About Not Wanting Walmart Poems,"

Cincinnati Review: "Dear Interviewer, Who Asked Me to Explain My Job at the Pool Hall,"

The Collagist: "Dear Editor, Who Wished Me Luck Placing My Poems Elsewhere"

Diode: "Dear Editor of Esteemed Midwestern Journal,"; "Dear Editors of Esteemed and Tiny Journals,"; "Dear Editor Sipping Wine the Color of Posh,"

Heavy Feather Review: "Dear Editor, Who Sent Me a Rejection Letter on Christmas,"

Indianapolis Review: "Dear Editor, I Did Not Go to AWP."

Lily Poetry Review: "Dear Editors, Who Didn't Send Me Interesting Rejection Letters,"

Limestone Review: "Dear Managing Editor of Esteemed Kentucky Poetry Journal, Who Wrote, 'We Have Completed the Selections for Our Spring Issue, and the Editors Have Not Recommended Your Work for Publication. However,'"

Rascal: "Dear Kind Editor, Who Accepted My Essay: 'Dear Editor, Who Wished Me Luck Placing my Poems Elsewhere,' in 17 Hours. I Am So Happy, Because Where Is Elsewhere Anyways? Someplace Very Far Away? Or Most Likely Too Often Exactly Where I Live?"; "Dear Editor, Who Wrote, 'We Have Decided Not to Select Any from This Batch. Best of Luck Finding Homes for Them,'"

Rogue Agent: "Dear HR Person from Health South Who Called,"

San Pedro River Review: "Dear Editor, Who Said Please No Third-Rate Raymond Carver Imitations,"

Stirring Lit: "Dear Editor, Who Returned My Essay Covered with Sticky Notes,"

"Dear Editor of Poetry Journals Named After Famous Cities," appeared in the anthology *Alongside We Travel: Contemporary Poets on Autism* (2019 NYQ Books)

All of these pieces should be considered works of fiction except where they are not.

In "Dear Editor, Who Said We Love Your Piece but Think It Could Be Improved by a Few Suggestions and Then Generously Gave them and Said If You Decide to Revise It, We'd Love to See it Again," the following lines are taken from Shakespeare's *Richard II*:

"A thousand, thousand sighs to save,
For you have but mistook me all this while:
I live with bread like you."

and

"Cover your heads and mock not flesh and blood
With solemn reverence: throw away respect,
Tradition, form and ceremonious duty."

In "Dear HR Person from Health South Who Called," the lines
"Work without Hope draws nectar in a sieve,/ And Hope without
an object cannot live" are taken from William Coleridge's poem
"Work Without Hope"

Various terms, definitions, psychological definitions, historical facts
and such were gathered from common internet sources and are not
meant to be taken as original scholarship or research.

CPSIA information can be obtained
at www.ICGtesting.com
Printed in the USA
LVHW090834041119
636238LV00008B/995/P